VICTORY!

THE STANLEY LONG
DEVOTIONAL BOOK

Foreword by Mark Hopkins

Compiled & Edited by Tim Ragan

Cover Photo by Rob Gribbin

Taken April 16, 2018, on a global missions survey trip to Togo, Africa, where Stanley's daughter, Meredith, now serves the Lord.

DEDICATION

Dedicated to the life, ministry, and legacy of our friend, Stanley Long.
Thank you for always pointing us to the victory we have in Christ!

To Kelle Long—you are greatly loved! Thank you for your joyful spirit,
faith-filled determination, overwhelming kindness, and incredibly sweet tea.

To the past, present, and future staff of Camp Eagle in Fincastle, Virginia:
As Stan said, "Go into the unreal world and be real!"

Thank you to the many friends who contributed your sermon notes,
staff meeting notes, audio sermon files, and other teachings.
This collection is only possible because of your help.

And most importantly,
"Thanks be to God, Who gives us the victory through our Lord Jesus Christ!"
1 CORINTHIANS 15:57

CONTENTS

CONTENTS

FOREWORD

Occasionally, you encounter a person who gets more accomplished in twenty-four hours than some do in a month…Stanley Long was that kind of man. I nicknamed him "The Mighty Doer." He was a modern-day Nehemiah who knew how to hold the shovel in one hand and a sword in the other while living singularly focused on God's assignment. As a beloved husband, father of nine children, and minister of the Gospel, he poured both the Word of God and his life into the next generation. Thousands of young people know Christ as their Lord and Savior through his Spirit-filled ministry, and hundreds have answered the call to make disciples with their lives. He was a man who made a definitive, unmistakable difference for Christ.

We had the privilege of being fellow pastors together and friends for over a decade. During that time, we shed tears, laughed, took on spiritual battles side-by-side, and enjoyed the victories God gave "in season" and "out of season." He was a man of continual vision, seeing what many could never see because He walked with the "eyes of faith." He was a man of vehement passion because the Bible "burned in his heart like a consuming fire." He was a man of child-like wonder who could have fun anytime, anywhere, even in the middle of the storm, yet his work ethic was unparalleled. He despised the "status quo" and habitually called believers to take "higher ground."

A love for God and a love for people was his passion. He wept, invested in, prayed for, and equipped people to make Christ their lives. Every day when I look at the framed copy of his favorite hymn, "Victory in Jesus," that his wife Kelle gave me after his passing, I'm reminded of I Corinthians 15:57 that he quoted regularly: "But thanks be to God, who gives us the victory through our Lord Jesus Christ." Stanley lived in victory by the grace of God and spent his waking moments trying to help others experience the same.

Preaching Stanley's funeral was one of the most challenging yet glorious things I've ever had the privilege of doing. Difficult because the passing of my Gospel comrade was deeply painful; glorious because I've preached very few funerals where someone had his testimony. He "fought the good fight" and "finished well" with a zeal unhindered. I want to do the same as I look to the Lord Jesus, His celestial kingdom, and the faithful lives of the mighty men of valor who have gone before me.

With sincere appreciation,

Mark Hopkins

NOW THAT'S VICTORY!

"Yet in all these things we are more than conquerors through Him Who loved us."

ROMANS 8:37

When children are divided for a game and one team has more players than the other, someone inevitably shouts, "That's not fair!" When numbers seem to be lopsided, we automatically assume some injustice or disadvantage.

At first glance, we may be tempted to say the same thing about being a Christian. The enemies who oppose followers of Jesus seem to outnumber us by a wide margin. We are opposed from within by our sinful nature (characterized by our self-centered desires), by Satan (who wants to steal God's glory), and by the world system (trying to conform us to its mold). But all of these enemies combined stand *ZERO* chance to defeat our Savior and His finished work on the cross! When we surrendered to Christ, we became "more than conquerors through Him Who loved us." (Romans 8:37)

Our sinful nature is powerless and defeated through Christ! Romans 6:6 says, "Knowing this, that our old man was crucified with Him, that the body of sin might be done away with, that we should no longer be slaves of sin." We do not become *sinless*, but as we become more like Christ, we do begin to *sin less*. We now have the power to say "no" to sin when temptation attacks. Those without Christ cannot say "no" because they are slaves of sin. But servants of God are no longer slaves to sin because we have a new Master— the Lord Jesus Christ! (Romans 6:22) Now *that's* victory!

Satan is also a defeated foe! (Revelation 12:9-12) Before salvation, we reflected Satan's characteristics (John 8:44), but after salvation, our characteristics have become like Christ's. Those characteristics are evidence of our salvation; evidence that Satan has lost his power over the Christian. Now *that's* victory!

Finally, the world is a defeated foe! (1 John 5:4-5) The world and all its systems have no more dominion over the Christian when he walks in victory with the Lord. There is no power in the world great enough to conform the Christian who has been transformed into the image of Jesus Christ! (Romans 12:1-2) Now *that's* victory! There is no hope for God's enemies when we choose victory in Christ! Praise God!

WALK IN VICTORY ... *One of my favorite songs is "Victory in Jesus." If you know it, sing it out loud to close your time today! If not, look up the words and meditate on these victorious truths!*

A LIFE OF INTEGRITY

"The Lord was with Joseph, and he was a successful man … And his master saw that the Lord was with him and that the Lord made all he did to prosper in his hand. So Joseph found favor in his sight, and served him…"

GENESIS 39:2-4

Integrity is one of those traits we appreciate in others but would prefer others not demand it of us. Why is that? We appreciate the benefits of being surrounded by people of integrity, but building a life of integrity is something else entirely! The idea of integrity comes from a root word meaning "intact." A person of integrity is morally intact, emotionally undivided, mentally unbroken, whole in purpose, and undamaged in character. This is a high calling!

Integrity is hard work and often encounters great temptation and opposition. In Genesis 39, we drop in on the Joseph story after his brothers have sold him into slavery. As a slave in Egypt, Joseph has a choice—become bitter and angry or remain "intact" as a man of integrity. Genesis 39 offers a snapshot of Joseph's life of integrity while serving as a slave in Potiphar's house, then as the overseer of Potiphar's house, then as a prisoner, and finally as the supervisor of the prisoners. Despite many difficult circumstances and unjust treatment, Joseph's integrity remains "intact." How is this possible?

Joseph understood that a life of integrity is built on clearly-defined standards. His standards were solidified. (v.9) He knew what he stood for and why he must remain morally intact. He knew his life reflected his trust in God, so to betray his standards—especially in front of idolatrous Egyptians—was to betray God. Joseph stood for his standards regardless of the circumstances. (vv.1-2, 21-23) Today, people often evolve their standards to fit who they are with, what they are doing, or how it might benefit them! We truly are a society overrun by cowardly chameleons.

Despite being far from home and having zero accountability to live a life pleasing to the Lord, Joseph maintained the standards based on his faith in the God of Abraham, Isaac, and Jacob. He refused to adopt the "culturally acceptable" standards of his Egyptian household. How do we know this? His standards were spoken. (v.9) Joseph was not afraid to make his convictions known, and God honored him for this! (vv.2-3, 5, 21-23) Would you like to live within God's blessing? Live God's way! But wait—like Joseph, once your standards are spoken, they will be meticulously nitpicked and methodically challenged!

4

Joseph's standards would not be swayed. He understood that compromising his integrity would be "great wickedness" against the Lord! (v.9) Striving for integrity means you will often stand alone (v.11), stand in scorn (vv.13-19), and stand in shame (v.19-20) because integrity often attracts the scrutiny of the enemy. Our enemy hates anything that glorifies God and inspires worship! This is one of the reasons a life of integrity brings the Savior's blessing!

As the enemy presses against the Christian's life of integrity, God continually redeems trials and temptations by blessing His loyal followers through whatever circumstances the enemy tries to manufacture. (See the story of Job.) Joseph's standards demonstrated his loyalty to God, and God rewarded his great faith by blessing everything he did!

WALK IN VICTORY ... *Are you living a life of integrity? Read the conclusion to Joseph's life of integrity in Genesis 50:15-23.*

A BURDEN FOR PRAYER

"And let us not grow weary while doing good,
for in due season we shall reap if we do not lose heart."

GALATIANS 6:9

Prayer is hard work. The Apostle Paul himself believed this! "Now I beg you, brethren, through the Lord Jesus Christ, and through the love of the Spirit, that you *strive together with me in prayers* to God for me." (Romans 15:30, emphasis added) To "strive" (that is, "struggle" or "fight") is a strong word when we're talking about prayer. Don't *just* pray, but *WRESTLE* in prayer! When you pray, don't just talk! *FIGHT!*

This is a healthy mindset to have because we are often tempted away from prayer. Paul's recommendation in Romans 15:30 is to remember that we pray "through the Lord Jesus Christ and through the love of the Spirit." In other words, we have been given access through Christ and power through the Spirit! We have everything we need to be effective, praying Christians!

But even with access and power, we sometimes lack motivation. We lack a *burden* for prayer. We allow our tiredness, our schedule, our thought-life, or our emotions to distract us away from the hard, humble work of prayer. Other burdens simply outweigh our burden for prayer. Against Paul's instruction in Galatians 6:9, we "grow weary while doing good." We give up on praying because a previous prayer (in our estimation) "didn't work." Either God said "no" or we never sensed any movement in the situation. We gave up! We grew weary in doing good. We forgot that we are in the midst of a battle and completely lost sight of the spiritual warfare waging around us.

But there is good news in the back half of verse 9, "In due season we shall reap if we do not lose heart." What if we *do not* lose heart in our praying? What if we *refused* to give up on prayer? "In due season, we shall reap…" There's no time to be weary! We cannot faint in the battle. We must grow desperate for prayer! If we desire to see the spiritual fruit of our labor, we must persevere in tending the garden of our soul with patient prayer. And as far as I can tell, there is only one way to give fresh weight to a burden for prayer—keep on praying!

WALK IN VICTORY… *Do you have a desperate burden for prayer? Pray and ask God to restore your burden for prayer!*

ENLISTING IN THE LORD'S ARMY

"You therefore must endure hardship as a good soldier of Jesus Christ. No one engaged in warfare entangles himself with the affairs of this life, that he may please him who enlisted him as a soldier."

2 TIMOTHY 2:3-4

When a sinner receives Jesus Christ as Lord and Savior, he is enlisting in the Lord's army. That means *every* Christian is a soldier of the cross! Therefore, like a well-trained soldier, the Christian must determine to be prepared, disciplined, and fit to accomplish the objectives of his Commanding Officer. In 2 Timothy 2:3-4, Paul uses the analogy of a soldier to describe the privilege and duty each Christian has to his Commander, the Lord Jesus Christ.

First, Christianity is not a life of ease. Paul encourages Timothy to "endure hardship." Why is this a command? Because our old sinful nature loves the easy way, but the Christian must determine to endure hardship in this world because we no longer fit in with the world system. Our goals, desires, and even citizenship are not of this world! (Ephesians 2:19) But as we determine to endure hardship, God gives us fulfillment, peace, and abundant joy!

Second, Christianity is a life of disciplined freedom. When Paul writes, "No one engaged in warfare entangles himself with the affairs of this life," (v.4) he is reminding us that good soldiers must determine to remain effective fighters in the spiritual battle. Receiving Christ as Lord gave us freedom from the bondage of sin, Satan, and the world! We are free to serve God! Determined soldiers of the cross exercise their freedom with great discipline—they do not sell out for cheap distractions!

Finally, Christianity is a life committed to pleasing the God Who has enlisted us into His army. When we understand that God loved us while we were still His enemies (Romans 5:8), joyful obedience should explode out of our thankful hearts! We now live in a privileged position as His son-soldiers! He has enlisted us through the blood of His Son (Ephesians 1:7), so as we engage in the spiritual battle, He will never leave nor forsake His troops. (Hebrews 13:5) What a privilege!

WALK IN VICTORY ... *Is your life as a soldier of Jesus Christ entangled in any way with the "civilian affairs" of this life rather than focusing on pleasing the Savior?*

Look up the hymn, "Am I a Soldier of the Cross" by Isaac Watts and reflect on the questions posed and declarations made in these rich lyrics!

A GOOD SOLDIER KNOWS HIS GEAR

"Finally, my brethren, be strong in the Lord and in the power of His might. Put on the whole armor of God, that you may be able to stand against the wiles of the devil."

EPHESIANS 6:10-11

Have you ever wondered why so many action movies feature main characters who are so ill-equipped for battle? Some shirtless guy runs around taking on entire armies with nothing but a big knife and a bad attitude. While it makes for compelling fiction, a good soldier would never run into a battle without his gear! For the Christian, our gear is even more important! As Paul reminds us, "For we do not wrestle against flesh and blood, but against principalities, against powers, against the rulers of the darkness of this age, against spiritual hosts of wickedness in the heavenly places. Therefore, take up the whole armor of God, that you may be able to withstand in the evil day, and having done all, to stand." (Ephesians 6:12-13) If we are going to "stand firm" (which is the main command of Ephesians 6:10-20), we need to become well-acquainted with the spiritual armory of the Lord Jesus!

Belt of Truth (v.14) – Just as the belt holds all of the gear in place, the absolute truth of God's Word is our foundation for living! It should be read, studied, and practiced daily because it is *TRUE!* (John 17:17) Jesus Himself is the truth (John 14:6), and His life teaches us how to live "full of grace and truth." (John 1:14) Do you want to know the truth? Know Jesus and His Word!

Breastplate of Righteousness (v.14) – Thanks be to God we have been given the righteousness of our Lord Jesus Christ! We call this "justification." A right relationship with God without condemnation gives us the ability to serve God and protects us from the accusations of the enemy. (Romans 5:1, 8:1)

Feet Shod with the Gospel of Peace (v.15) – Feet are your foundation, and what could be more foundational than the Good News that you have peace with God? This Good News gives us stability and mobility. We stand firm against the world's pushback and mobilize the Gospel message to the lost!

Shield of Faith (v.16) – "Above all" Paul tells us in verse 16, take up the shield of faith because with it we are protected from the lies of our enemy which blaze with the fire of hell. Faith declares, "I believe *You*, Lord!" That is the only true defense against the enemy's lies! Remember this, too—faith says you are not alone! The shield of faith is a shield wall, friends! As we stand shoulder-to-shoulder in the same Gospel with the same faith, we are protected on all sides! This is why Christians cannot operate in isolation. We need every faith to be *active* because we need every shield raised as one!

Helmet of Salvation (v.17) – Romans 12:1-2 tells us about the necessity of a renewed mind. A mind protected by the helmet of salvation means we become spiritually alert! Instead of living with a deadened mind, doubting mind, deceived mind, double mind, or discouraged mind, we live with the mind of Christ! His mind in us is alive, trusting, true, righteous, pure, and courageous! (Philippians 2:5, 4:8)

Sword of the Spirit (v.17) – When the Holy Spirit unsheathes the Word of God, He gives direction, purpose, and instruction. He also convicts our hearts of sin and soundly defeats God's enemies with God's truth to make us holy. (John 16:7-11)

Prayer (v.18) – Communion with our Commanding Officer—what a privilege! There is nothing left untouched through prayer. In prayer, mature faith is developed through fellowship and access as we focus our hearts on the sufficiency of the Lord and the deep neediness of our souls!

WALK IN VICTORY ... *Which part of your gear was a good reminder for your heart and mind today? Do not go into battle unprepared! Gear up, soldier of the cross!*

A GOOD SOLDIER
DEVELOPS A TENACIOUS SPIRIT

"Be of good courage and He shall strengthen your heart,
all you who hope in the LORD."

PSALM 31:24

When I was a child, several bullies lived in my neighborhood. Each had his own way of intimidating, but all of them had one thing in common—they ruled by fear! Despite their cowardly tactics, these bullies knew they could control anyone they intimidated. But if you were courageous and refused to give in to their demands, they no longer had any control over you!

A victorious principle needed in the life of a good soldier is the development of a tenacious spirit. The word tenacious means "not easily pulled apart; tough; persistent to maintain something valued or worthwhile." When the Apostle Paul wrote his closing remarks to the church in Corinth, he used a word that literally translates, "act like men." (1 Corinthians 16:13) At first glance, this verse might sound like a strange command (especially if you were a female church member in Corinth), but I like it! "Act like men!" In other words, if we are going to be good soldiers of the Lord Jesus Christ, we must develop maturity, courage, and faithful devotion to what is right in the face of great fear. We must not be intimidated or controlled. This is a command for both men and women in the Lord's army who desire to develop a tenacious spirit!

Enemies of the cross of Christ will always try to control Christians through fear and intimidation—the same cowardly tactics used by my neighborhood bullies. Satan is a bully. He knows he can control us when we act in fear. He tempts us to be afraid of sharing the Gospel, fearful of praying in public, or anxious about standing up for biblical truth in our school or workplace. He will use fear of our neighbors, friends, or family if it can keep us from being courageous for the Lord Jesus. But the Christian who develops a tenacious spirit cannot be bullied because he is as bold as a lion for the cause of Jesus Christ! (Proverbs 28:1) Do not let fear make you let go of God!

WALK IN VICTORY ... How have you let fear call the shots in your life recently? Where do you need to repent and develop a tenacious spirit of obedience to the Lord Jesus Christ? Write out Proverbs 28:1 on a notecard and put it somewhere you will see it often.

A GOOD SOLDIER
DEVELOPS TACTICAL STABILITY

"Stand fast therefore in the liberty by which Christ has made us free, and do not be entangled again with a yoke of bondage."

GALATIANS 5:1

On July 21, 1861, one of the Civil War's most celebrated soldiers earned his famous nickname. Despite a heavy enemy attack, General Thomas Jackson's overmatched brigade held a strategic hilltop position during the battle of First Manassas (also known as "Bull Run"). A fellow Confederate general, trying to rally his troops, pointed to Jackson's soldiers and cried, "There is Jackson standing like a stone wall! Let us determine to die here and we will conquer." From that day forward, Thomas Jackson was called General "Stonewall" Jackson. What a nickname!

Look at 1 Corinthians 16:13a, "Watch, stand fast [firm] in the faith…" For a Christian to be a good soldier of the Lord Jesus Christ, he must develop tactical stability. In warfare, the army holding the high ground is most likely to win the battle. As Christians, we hold the "high ground" when we build our lives on the firm foundation of the Lord Jesus Christ—standing on the principles and promises of God's Word. Notice the Apostle Paul tells us in 1 Corinthians 16:13 to, "Stand fast [firm] in *the* faith" (emphasis added). Paul does not want us to build our lives on just any old beliefs. Here, *"the* faith" refers to the promises about the finished work of Christ and the principles of Christlike living. By building on God's Word, a firm foundation is cemented under our feet. We can stand firm on a strong, biblical foundation when the enemy attacks or the trials of life confront us.

Without a biblical foundation, Ephesians 4:14 says we will be tossed around and carried off by every new belief that blows through popular culture, manipulated by every fleeting fairytale, and ensnared by every sweet-sounding falsehood. A good soldier knows better. Let us determine to stand firm on the high ground of God's Word! Only the truth provides tactical stability to live victoriously!

WALK IN VICTORY ... *Is your life built on the firm foundation of God's Word, or do you trust other voices to tell you what is true? Meditate on these verses today: Deuteronomy 31:6; Isaiah 41:10; Joshua 1:9; Psalm 27:1; 1 Corinthians 15:58; Philippians 1:27*

A GOOD SOLDIER
DEVELOPS TOTAL SELFLESSNESS

"Let all that you do be done with love."

1 CORINTHIANS 16:14

You have probably heard the saying, "Look out for number one!" That is, make sure you look out for *yourself*. After all, everyone else is doing the same thing, right? "No one else is going to make you a priority, so you better take good care of yourself!" Sadly, we are all innately selfish, self-centered, and self-serving. This is the common heart attitude of the sin nature, and it makes us our own worst enemy! Our selfish desires, unfulfilled wants, and uncontrolled ambitions with their "me, myself, and I" mentality fail us in the end because we can never be truly satisfied through selfish gain.

But thanks be to God! He has rendered that selfish sin nature powerless at the cross of Christ! We are no longer slaves to this way of living! Once we receive Jesus as Lord and Savior, the Holy Spirit—our *new* nature—fills us and enables us with the power to serve others through the love of Christ! The Holy Spirit gives and motivates this love so we might serve others as a demonstration of our new nature in Christ. Such selflessness cannot be faked or artificially manufactured! This supernatural love proves we are truly children of God! (1 John 2:5-6) If developing total selflessness eliminates the need to "Look out for number one," our new question becomes "Who should we serve?"

Serve the One and Only: *Jesus Christ* ... In Mark 12:30, Jesus said, "And you shall love the Lord your God with all your heart, with all your soul, with all your mind, and with all your strength. This is the first commandment." We demonstrate our new nature of total selflessness through our love for Him!

Serve One Another: *Fellow Believers* ... Jesus once told His disciples, "By this all will know that you are My disciples, if you have love for one another." (John 13:35) The new nature of love and total selflessness distinguishes the Christian from those without Christ.

Serve Anyone: *The Lost* ... When Christ reigns in our lives, we will develop the desire to serve those without Christ, hoping to see them receive the Lord. The natural man hates those who oppose him, but the Holy Spirit enables the Christian to love those who oppose him. When Christ is in charge of our lives, total selflessness will be the overflow! (See Matthew 5:44)

WALK IN VICTORY ... *Is there someone you are struggling to love well right now?*

A GOOD SOLDIER
DEVELOPS TRAINED SIGHT

"And do this, knowing the time, that now it is high time to awake out of sleep;
for now our salvation is nearer than when we first believed. The night is far spent,
the day is at hand. Therefore let us cast off the works of darkness,
and let us put on the armor of light."

ROMANS 13:11-12

A soldier who desires to live a life of victory and keep himself from being overtaken by the enemy must develop "trained sight." When finishing his first letter to the church at Corinth, Paul states, "*Watch*, stand fast in the faith, be brave, be strong." (1 Corinthians 16:13, emphasis added) The thought here is to stay alert or "wide awake," remaining keenly aware of our surroundings to recognize the attacks of the enemy. Notice that a watchful disposition is the first posture we must take! Before you could ever hope to stand firm in the faith or be brave or be strong, you must be aware.

God's creation can teach us many lessons about staying alert. The deer is a great illustration of the way believers should be keenly aware of our surroundings. When a deer, especially a young buck, is feeding as he moves through the woods, he keeps a keen eye on everything around him. He is especially alert to predators who might seek his harm. If he senses the slightest danger, he's out of there! His eyes are constantly scanning his surroundings to ensure the enemy is not approaching. But every good hunter knows when that young buck is most vulnerable. During mating season, that usually, cautious buck loses his mind! He lets down his guard, is easily distracted, and chases every young doe that crosses his path. He falls for the temptations of his flesh and loses all awareness of any present danger.

Christians can certainly look like that young buck, falling for the enemy's tactics of distraction and sensuality. We let down our guard and become unaware instead of alert to temptation. Are your eyes wide awake to the temptations around you?

WALK IN VICTORY ... *Do you recognize the tactics of the enemy who seeks to ensnare you in a life of sinful compromise? (See John 10:10) Pray and ask the Lord to deliver you from the lies of the enemy and give you the strength and awareness to say "No!" to every temptation.*

A GOOD SOLDIER DEVELOPS
TRANSCENDENT STRENGTH

"I can do all things through Christ who strengthens me."

PHILIPPIANS 4:13

"It's a bird! It's a plane! No, it's Superman!"

Everyone loves the idea of a superhero! Someone who uses heroic strength to fight for good and triumph over evil. We often think this kind of strength is fictional. "If only someone like that existed…"

Did you realize the Lord has equipped every Christian with supernatural strength to fight for good and triumph over evil? It's true! No, this strength cannot stop a steaming locomotive or enable us to leap over tall buildings in a single bound, but it was strong enough to raise Jesus from the dead!

The Bible says this transcendent (or "superior") strength is accessible to every Christian! As soldiers of the cross, we develop this strength by "working out." (Philippians 2:12-13) Does God expect us to start lifting weights? Not in this case. We will never find spiritual strength in our own power. Christ not only calls us to be strong, He gives us the ability to be strong! "For *it is God who works in you* both to will and to do for His good pleasure." (Philippians 2:13, emphasis added).

To be effective soldiers for Christ, we must live through the transcendent strength of the Holy Spirit within us, realizing all our strength comes from His supply. Paul puts it this way, "Be strong *in the Lord*, and *in the power* of *His might*." (Ephesians 6:10, emphasis added)

Every soldier wants to be powerful in battle, but the only way we can wield God's strength and power is to surrender our own. Once we understand our *inability* to live the Christian life, we are finally in a position to access the transcendent strength the Holy Spirit provides!

WALK IN VICTORY … *How often do you feel frustrated by your inability to live the Christian life? Confess your inability to the Lord Jesus Christ and surrender control of your life to His Holy Spirit today! (See Romans 12:1-2)*

A MOUNTAIN-TOP EXPERIENCE

"Then the fire of the Lord fell and consumed the burnt sacrifice ..."

1 KINGS 18:37

One of the best things about living in southwest Virginia is the mountains. Some of the greatest outdoor experiences of my life happened in those mountains. A "mountain-top experience" is what we often call a special move of God in our lives. In the Bible, mountain-top meetings with God are significant. If you studied all of the mountain-top experiences in the Bible, several consistent characteristics pop up in every account! Let's examine one of those stories today. [Read 1 Kings 18:16-46]

The Mountain Top is a Place of Choice! (v.21) The mountain is a place where you are faced with a choice—will you follow God or not? This is not only seen in the Elijah story, but as far back as Genesis 3, Genesis 8, Genesis 22, and Numbers 3. Mountains are a place to declare your allegiance to the Lord!

The Mountain Top is a Place of Consecration! (v.22) To consecrate means to dedicate something for worship. The mountain is a place to dedicate your life as a living sacrifice to the Lord! (Romans 12:1-2) It is a place where loyalty is declared before it is tested in the valley below.

The Mountain Top is a Place of Challenge! (vv.23-24) A mountain-top experience with God will challenge you in your Christian walk. It is a place where the Lord shows Himself strong and He strengthens our faith! The mountain top gives you the clearest view of the challenges behind and the challenges ahead.

The Mountain Top is a Place of Calling! (vv.27-38) The mountain is a place to cry out to the Lord! It is also a place where God calls us to service. In the ancient world, mountains were a place to commune with God and gain clarity. The same is true for us! Cry out to the Lord in prayer! (Psalm 3:4)

The Mountain Top is a Place of Confirmation! (v.39) What needs to be confirmed on the mountain? God alone is worthy of our worship! When we see the wondrous works of our great God, our faith is strengthened and we are encouraged to live for Him! When was the last time you climbed the mountain to meet with God?

***WALK IN VICTORY** ... Are you consistently meeting with God in the Word and prayer? Consider scheduling a special "mountain-top" retreat to meet with God for an extended time.*

DERAILING DISCOURAGEMENT

"What are you doing here, Elijah?"

1 KINGS 19:9

Have you ever been discouraged in your Christian walk? Every one of us would have to say, "YES!" While there are many Psalms and Bible stories where we could examine characteristics of discouragement, I am always amazed to revisit the story in 1 Kings 19 where God Himself shows us how He helped Elijah, one of His chief servants, derail discouragement in his life.

[Read 1 Kings 19]

I want us to note a few things about discouragement from this story:

(1) It came at the pinnacle of Elijah's ministry. He had just had his mountain-top showdown with the prophets of Baal. God is victorious, but Elijah is worn out. The adrenaline has worn off and it was time to re-enter the valley.

(2) It came verbally from an enemy. Many times, we are discouraged by what people say (or supposedly say) about us. We tend to "tune out" the voice of the Holy Spirit when negative people loom large in our lives.

(3) It affected Elijah mentally (he forgot about God), emotionally (he became suicidal), physically (he was worn out), and spiritually (he doubted God). He was under attack in every way! As a result, he abandoned God's perspective on the situation and he was no longer living in light of God's glorious victory.

How did God derail Elijah's discouragement? And how can we adopt some of the same tactics to derail discouragement in our own lives?

REST – Go to bed and eat right! (vv.5-8) Our physical bodies are not separated and isolated from our spiritual state. If you neglect the material part of you, the spiritual part will suffer too! Notice that God addresses this "easy" step first. This is always a good place to begin derailing discouragement!

RETREAT – Get alone with God. (vv.8-9) Elijah headed to the mountain of God. When discouragement comes, we *must* seek solitude with God. Even the Lord Jesus practiced this spiritual discipline! (Matthew 14:1-13; Mark 6:30-32; Luke 5:16, 6:12-13) Time spent alone with God is never truly alone!

REFLECT – Gaze at the actions of God. (vv.10-12) When we need encouragement, we must reflect on *all* the things that God has done for us in the past and what God is doing in the present! An inward focus will not defeat discouragement—it feeds feelings of discouragement! (see vv. 10, 14)

One of the great comforts in the Christian walk is that it's not "up to us" to figure things out. God is at work (whether we see it or not), and we have the privilege of joining Him in His work!

RENEW – Go to the Word of God. (vv.9, 12-15) "The word of the LORD came to Elijah…" Remember, discouragement is a mindset that is defeating us in many ways. The only way to change a mindset is through God's Word. (Romans 12:1-2) Friends, family, positive thinking, and professional help cannot change you—only God can do that! A "right mind" is the work of God's Spirit in a wholly surrendered life! (Romans 8:6)

RE-COMMIT – Go and do the will of God! (vv.15-19) Obeying God might not "solve" the emotional aspect of discouragement immediately, but your emotions *will* have to "catch up" to your actions eventually. Doing what is wrong or self-indulgent will not cure a discouraged heart! Continue to do what is right—especially when you do not feel like it!

WALK IN VICTORY ... *How do you typically engage your discouragement? Do you have spiritually healthy or unhealthy patterns and methods of engagement? As you look to "re-commit," here are a few starting points: 1 Thessalonians 4:3, 5:18; Luke 9:23; James 1:5; Proverbs 3:5-6; 1 Peter 2:11-15; Ephesians 5:15-17; Hebrews 10:36*

A PRAYER FOR DELIVERANCE

"In the day of my trouble, I will call upon You, for You will answer me."

PSALM 86:7

On the dark night of December 26, 1860, Union Major Robert Anderson slipped his blue-clad troops into an unfinished Fort Sumter located in the Charleston harbor. South Carolina had just seceded from the Union, and Anderson saw Fort Sumter as the only place where his artillery brigade could successfully hold the harbor. After several tense months, Jefferson Davis, President of the Confederate States of America, ordered General P.T. Beauregard to take Fort Sumter by force—the first shots of the American Civil War were fired. Early bombardment of the fort proved ineffective, but 34 hours of relentless assault ultimately forced the Union troops to surrender.

We have an enemy blasting us from every angle—hoping to strike where we are most vulnerable. We need deliverance! In Psalm 86, King David begins with the picture of a toddler asking his towering father to bow down and listen to him. If we are going to seek deliverance from the enemy's onslaught, we must understand that we are needy people. If we desire victory in the battle, we must humbly seek the Lord! According to Psalm 86, He is the One Who preserves and supports (v.2), pours out mercy (v.3), fills us with joy (v.4), lifts us up (v.4), treats us with goodness and forgiveness (v.5), listens for our call (vv.6-7), and defeats any rivals! (vv.8-10) This is our victorious God! "If God is for us, who can be against us?" (Romans 8:31)

God seems to be doing most of the heavy lifting in Psalm 86! Do we have any responsibilities in this? Of course, we do! We must approach God with a spirit of humble submission and obedience—that is, an "undivided" inner man. (v.11) Whole-hearted submission and obedience lead us to a proper perspective of God. This perspective is overwhelmed with thankfulness and praise as we recognize His goodness and merciful deliverance! (vv.12-13)

How does this work out practically? You will endure hardship and experience opposition, but our experiential knowledge of God's character helps us endure hardship. (vv.14-15) David knew this. He had "been there, done that." He knew how to pray in dangerous times! "Oh, turn to me, and have mercy on me! Give Your strength to Your servant… Because You, Lord, have helped me and comforted me." (vv.16-17) Do you need help in the midst of bombardment? Will you humbly seek God's victorious deliverance?

WALK IN VICTORY ... *Pray through Psalm 86 today.*

ASK! NO, *YOU* ASK!

"Now this is the confidence that we have in Him, that if we ask anything according to His will, He hears us. And if we know that He hears us, whatever we ask, we know that we have the petitions that we have asked of Him."

1 JOHN 5:14-15

As a father of nine children, I've noticed that some of them are reluctant to ask for things. The reluctant ones often try to prompt their younger siblings to make the request on their behalf. For instance, "Ask Mom if we can get some ice cream!" Why is it so hard for some children to just ask? I noticed the same thing growing up with five sisters and one brother. There was always a debate about who would ask our parents for something. The exchange would go something like this: one would coax another saying, "Ask!" The one being coaxed would return by saying, "No, *you* ask!" This exchange would go on and on until someone either did the asking or we abandoned the request altogether.

There are several reasons why children might not ask for something from a parent. They might not have total confidence in their parent's authority or ability to grant the request. Maybe they fear an upset or annoyed reaction to the request. Maybe they fear the request will be denied. Pride or stubbornness will keep some from humbling themselves to such an uncertain, vulnerable position. Funny enough, the only thing not considered is this—without asking, you can be certain you will *NOT* hear a "Yes!"

We might shake our heads at this scenario, but a child of God lacking a prayer life is far more ridiculous! Lack of prayer in a child of God reveals many of the same doubting problems listed above! According to 1 John 5:14-15, God's children can be confident that He hears *and* answers prayers! Rather than trying to establish the "rules" for our asking from these verses, engage the command to ASK! God is a good Father Who loves His children. He will guide your asking through His Word and His answers.

Like a good Father, our Lord is pleased when we trust Him for our needs. He is pleased by our humility in asking, and He is more than willing to provide for His children! Evaluate your prayer life. Examine the reasons why children often avoid making requests. Are any of these previously mentioned reasons keeping you from praying to your Heavenly Father?

WALK IN VICTORY *... Consider starting a prayer journal to write the things you need to ask of the Lord. You will be amazed as you record the answers to your prayers!*

ABIDING IN CHRIST

"As the Father loved Me, I also have loved you; abide in My love."

JOHN 15:1

While the Lord was teaching His disciples in John 15, He outlines the necessity and fruitfulness of abiding in Christ and the "love-hate" reactions caused by abiding (or being "at home") in Christ. Abiding in Christ's overwhelming love provokes the enemies of the cross to hate anyone who finds a home in God's love.

In verses 9-17, "love" is mentioned nine times. In Christ, we are brought into the "shared love" of the Godhead. "As the Father loved Me, I also have loved you; abide in My love." (v.9) The Father loves the Son and the Son loves the Father. By abiding (that is, finding our home) in the Lord Jesus, we have been brought into the circle of God's love. How do we know we're "in?" By obeying Christ! (v.10) If we obey the Lord, it is because we love the Lord and desire to please Him. Obeying isn't the way into God's love—Christ is! But loving the Lord through obedient service demonstrates God's love in us! (1 John 4:7-8) Furthermore, abiding in the love of Christ causes us to love one another sacrificially. (vv.12-13,17) Our love for one another is yet another proof that we have made our home in the circle of God's love! When God's love dwells in us, we cannot help but love others the way God does! (v.13) And this is not a suggestion—it's a calling (v.16) and a command! (v.17)

In verses 18-27, "hate" is mentioned eight times. How does hate weasel its way in on all this love? "If the world hates you, you know that it hated Me before it hated you. If you were of the world, the world would love its own. Yet because you are not of the world..." (vv.18-19) Since abiding Christians now feel "at home" in the circle of God's love, guess where they no longer fit in? That's right—to be loved and accepted by God means you no longer feel "at home" among the enemies of the cross. Praise God! You might be hated by God's enemies, but God is greater than ALL of His enemies combined, and He hears our prayers in times of difficulty! (1 John 4:4-5) There is good news in the hate, however. We are hated for the sake of His name! "But all these things they will do to you for My name's sake..." (v.21) And like the early church in Acts 5:41, we can rejoice that we have been counted worthy to suffer hardship for the name of the Lord Jesus Christ! Even suffering is victorious in the confident refuge of His great love!

WALK IN VICTORY ... *Read all of John 15 and meditate on this rich chapter!*

ATTACK FROM WITHIN

"But a certain man named Ananias, with Sapphira his wife, sold a possession. And he kept back part of the proceeds, his wife also being aware of it, and brought a certain part and laid it at the apostles' feet."

ACTS 5:1-2

The attack of our enemy is relentless. In Acts 4 we see the enemy attack from *outside* the church through persecution. In many ways, this attack was a rallying point and brought great unity! But soon after, we see the attack from *within*—a devastating "first" in the early church.

An attack from within attacks God's character. God is loving, generous, and true. When Barnabas sold some land, he laid the profits at the apostles' feet as an act of sacrifice, service, and encouragement! It was not about him, and no one asked him to do it! (See Acts 4:32-37) His heart overflowed with the love of God! Conversely, Ananias and Sapphira did a similar act with impure motives and a deceptive story. Peter even claims they lied to God Himself! (5:3) They elevated themselves which meant they would be humbled by God.

This was also an attack on God's glory. Pride, the root of sin, always steals the glory from God, and God resists the proud. (James 4:6-10) Humility is recognizing we would have *NOTHING* without God's great grace, kindness, and love! Ananias and Sapphira wanted people to notice *them*, and they were willing to steal God's glory by exaggerating the level of their sacrifice.

The unity of the church also came under attack. Unity comes from purity— it cannot be won through any sinful means, especially lying. These attempts to artificially manufacture unity only create a false sense of unity that cannot last. Humility, purity, integrity, and transparency bring genuine unity because these qualities are rooted in *TRUTH*.

Finally, Ananias and Sapphira led an attack on God's grace. Though grace is always greater than our sin (Romans 5:20-21), grace never gives us a license to sin! (Romans 6:1-2) Sin is an affront to God's great grace! Continually harboring known sin and wanting to be used for God's service distorts the message of grace, and gives a stronghold to the enemy inside the camp. (See Joshua 7) By grace, we serve the Lord in Spirit and truth. Disregarding sin and thinking we are fit for service is a wrong view of our Lord. (2 Timothy 2:20-22)

WALK IN VICTORY ... *Prayerfully allow the Lord to examine your heart by meditating on 2 Timothy 2:20-22.*

ATTRIBUTES OF THE CRUCIFIED

"And when they had come to the place called Calvary, there they crucified Him..."

LUKE 23:33

George Müller understood the power and freedom of the crucified life. As an evangelist and the director of the Ashley Down Orphanage in Bristol, England (where he cared for over 10,000 orphans in his lifetime), Müller once remarked, "There was a day when I died; died to self, my opinions, preferences, tastes and will; died to the world, its approval or censure; died to the approval or blame even of my brethren or friends; and since then I have studied only to show myself approved unto God."

This is a perfect vision of the crucified life! But why should we desire to live a crucified life? And what does it look like to live a crucified life? Christ has commanded all His followers to live a cross-bearing life (Luke 9:23-24) and provided how we live crucified! (Galatians 2:20; Romans 6:6-7; Colossians 2:13-15) By reflecting on the seven statements made by the Lord Jesus when He was on the cross, we begin to see a picture of the foundational attributes of the crucified life.

MATTHEW 27:46 ... *"My God, My God, why have you forsaken me?"*

The crucified life understands the beauty of God's holiness, the ugliness of man's sin, and the radical obedience required to bridge the impossible gap between the two. The Lord Jesus was willing to suffer and give His life for the needs of others to accomplish God's will in redemption and restoration. Likewise, the crucified Christian recognizes the severity, costliness, and destruction of sin as well as the beauty of holy living.

LUKE 23:34 ... *"Father, forgive them, for they do not know what they do."*

The Lord Jesus did not play the victim as He hung on the cross. He was merciful to the unjust, not vengeful. Rather than blame those who caused His excruciating suffering, He seeks to forgive. The crucified Christian does not blame shift or seek revenge.

LUKE 23:43 ... *"Assuredly, I say to you, today you will be with Me in Paradise."*

Even as Christ is dying, He reaches out to comfort a suffering sinner with good news and meet the need of his eternal soul. The crucified Christian will also endure suffering, yet still finds hope in the eternal rather than focusing on the plight of the present.

LUKE 23:46 … *"Father, into Your hands I commit my Spirit!"*

In this beautiful and haunting declaration of faith, the crucified Christ places total trust in God. He accomplished the perfect will of the Father and was willing to trust God with the results. The crucified Christian completely yields all rights to God.

JOHN 19:26-27 … *"Woman, behold your son … Behold, your mother."*

Christ looks at two incredibly special people—Mary, His mother, and John, the beloved disciple—and gives them to each other. Even in immense pain and suffering, the Lord Jesus is concerned for the ones in His loving care. The crucified Christian, like Christ, loves others selflessly.

JOHN 19:28 … *"I thirst!"*

Christ, knowing that the job was done, takes a final drink before His dying declaration. John makes a prophetic connection to this request. Christ had experienced the spiritual thirst of man's disobedience, drank God's cup of suffering, and provided Living Water for the thirsty. The crucified Christian is thirsty for God.

JOHN 19:30 … *"It is finished!"*

The Lord Jesus sprints through the finish line. He does not "let up" as the end approaches because God *always* finishes what He starts! The crucified Christian pursues God's will until his life is over.

WALK IN VICTORY … *Does your life reflect the characteristics of a crucified life? Take time to meditate on George Müller's quote. Have you "died" to all these things?*

EARLY MORNING COMMUNION

"Now in the morning, having risen a long while before daylight, He went out and departed to a solitary place; and there He prayed."

MARK 1:35

Throughout His earthly ministry, our Lord prioritized communion with His Father. When we examine pivotal moments in the life and ministry of Jesus, we consistently find Him spending significant time in deep, prayerful communion with the Father. "The Son can do nothing of Himself, but what He sees the Father do." (John 5:19b) Jesus, the God-man, declares His dependence on the Father for direction, power, encouragement, and purpose. "Father, Tell Me what to do!" This was the cry of our Lord's heart!

In Mark 1, Jesus rises "a long while before daylight" for the singular purpose of communion with the Father. The day ahead would be full of ministry, but the morning before the ministry would be filled by the Father. In Luke 4:1-15, Jesus endures temptation as He prays and fasts in the desert for forty days before the inauguration of His earthly ministry. He prays all night and into the early morning before initiating His public ministry in Luke 4:42-44. He does the same thing in Luke 6:12-13 before calling the twelve as His disciples and again in Matthew 14 before walking across stormy water to a boatload of terrified disciples. Most famously, as the overture preceding the suffering of the cross, Jesus passionately communes with the Father in the Garden of Gethsemane with blood, sweat, and tears. (Mark 14:32-42)

If we believe the Father's will is perfect, His love overwhelming, and His plans holy and right, then our morning communion should be an *urgent* necessity! What other motivation do we need? What else could convince us if not the example of our Lord and Savior? Our actions betray what we believe in our hearts to be true. May our morning communion reveal our dependence on God, make us obedient servants, and fill us with the victorious joy of sonship!

WALK IN VICTORY *... Is daily communion with God a priority in your life?*

Consider these benefits – Strength (Psalm 1:1-2); Heard by God (Psalm 5:3);
Quieted Spirit (Psalm 46:10); Satisfaction (Psalm 90:14); Cleansing (Psalm 119:9);
Affirmation of Love (Psalm 143:8); Fresh Mercy (Lamentations 3:22-23);
Realigned Priorities (Matthew 6:33); Sustained Obedience (John 4:34)

CLOSE DOESN'T COUNT

"Be diligent to come to me quickly; for Demas has forsaken me, having loved this present world, and has departed for Thessalonica … Only Luke is with me."

2 TIMOTHY 4:9-11

It was Frank Robinson who coined the phrase, "Close don't count in baseball. Close only counts in horseshoes and hand grenades." Robinson had a long and successful career in Major League Baseball as a player, coach, and manager. His quote reflects that baseball tends to reduce every action to its result: runs, hits, RBIs, errors, and outs. There is no glory for coming close. A weakly hit groundout is scored the same way as a screaming line drive caught by the outstretched arm of a diving outfielder. Only the *result* matters.

In a brief closing line of 2 Timothy 4, the Apostle Paul tells us about a fellow worker named Demas who was once on the side of faith but deserted Paul and his ministry. We do not know much about Demas, but Paul reveals enough to serve as a warning that "close doesn't count."

"Demas has forsaken me … and departed for Thessalonica" … Demas was once a key part of Paul's traveling ministry team, and was likely with Paul in Rome. (Philemon 1:24; Colossians 4:14) The word Paul uses to describe his sudden departure suggests that Demas left Paul in a time of great need. Paul was in prison, facing a death sentence, and Demas chose to set sail for Thessalonica. There is no question Paul was deeply hurt and betrayed by Demas.

"Having loved this present world" … Not only did Demas physically abandon Paul, but he also spiritually deserted the Lord Jesus. This did not happen overnight—Demas had cultivated the wrong love. He chose the corrupt system of this world over what God has to offer. The spirit of Demas is still active in the world today through those who choose the temporary benefits of this world over the eternal riches of Christ. You cannot love the world and love God at the same time. (1 John 2:15-17)

"Only Luke is with me" … For every Demas, there is the choice to be a Luke. "The beloved physician" was a close friend of Paul and a traveling companion at the same time as Demas. (Colossians 4:14) Luke traveled extensively with Paul and faced many trials alongside the Apostle. It is evident from Dr. Luke's writing that he was not just close to Paul, but close to the Lord as well. Luke knew what Demas did not—close doesn't count! The result is what matters. Are you truly committed to the Lord Jesus?

WALK IN VICTORY … *In what ways are you harboring love for this present world?*

BROKENNESS

"I tell you, this man went down to his house justified…"

LUKE 18:14

A horse needs to be "broken" to be useful. Otherwise, it will never yield to the control of a rider. A broken horse is not unhappy or oppressed by its situation. In fact, it has never had more purpose in its entire life! By accepting the weight of a rider, the discipline of bit and bridle, and the direction of reigns, a broken horse is given care, comfort, nourishment, purpose, and protection! A wild, unbroken horse may still be powerful and beautiful, but a wild, unbroken human is a fool. There are no "free-roaming" Christians running around unbridled! When Jesus is Lord, the sinful will has been broken! God opposes the proud (or "unbroken") who refuse the weight of His Lordship, and in Luke 18:9-14, Jesus uses a parable of two praying men to teach us about the beauty of brokenness.

Luke 18:9 tells us that the Lord was speaking to a group of people who were self-righteous and looked down on anyone who didn't "measure up" to their standard of living. In Jesus' story, the religious man (a Pharisee) represented an unbroken spirit. "God, I thank You that I am not like other men— extortioners, unjust, adulterers, or even as this tax collector. I fast twice a week; I give tithes of all that I possess." (vv.11-12) He wanted God to know how incredible *he* was—never once mentioning the greatness of God or the plight of his sinful soul before a holy God! He had an unbroken soul. A soul without purpose, discipline, direction, nourishment, or a home.

Then Jesus introduces the broken man—a tax collector. This Jewish agent of Roman oppression represented everything wrong with Rome's occupation of the Promised Land. The scripture says this tax collector, standing far away from everyone else and refusing to lift his eyes from the floor, beat his chest in agony as he prayed, "God, be merciful to me a sinner!" (v.13) There is no self-reliance or self-righteousness in this man because he knew his spiritual condition. His heart is humble as he begs for mercy from a holy God! Then the Lord makes His point clear: "I tell you, this man went down to his house justified [right with God] rather than the other; for everyone who exalts himself will be humbled, and he who humbles himself will be exalted." (v.14) Which of these men are you today?

WALK IN VICTORY … *Are you broken for the Master's use or fighting for independence? Prayerfully meditate on these "unbroken" passages today: Psalm 138:6; Proverbs 3:34; Proverbs 29:23; Matthew 23:12; Luke 1:52; James 4:6; 1 Peter 5:5-6*

CAN'T GET NO SATISFACTION?

"Do not love the world ... For all that is in the world—the lust of the flesh, the lust of the eyes, and the pride of life—is not of the Father but is of the world..."

1 JOHN 2:15-17

Growing up, I heard a song where the singer exclaimed, "I can't get no satisfaction!" He then went on to describe all the ways that life had fallen short and left him unfulfilled. The pursuit of satisfaction might be one of the most common experiences in human history. While we are constantly seeking the next satisfying experience, the world fills our hungry life with unsatisfying junk that just makes us sick! Let's examine three false sources of satisfaction and then turn to the only true source of satisfaction, the Lord Jesus Christ!

"The Lust of the Flesh" ... This is the desire to experience everything! The "fear of missing out" drives everything you do because you are afraid that the one thing you skip will finally be the thing that satisfies your soul. Filled with empty pleasures, you rarely tell yourself "No," but you remain unsatisfied.

"The Lust of the Eyes" ... This is the desire to possess everything! Maybe "having it all" will fill the emptiness inside? King Solomon would laugh! He "surpassed all the kings of the earth in riches and wisdom" (2 Chronicles 9:22), but later wrote, "Therefore I hated life ... for all is vanity [emptiness] and grasping for the wind." (Ecclesiastes 2:17) No, "stuff" is empty too.

"The Pride of Life" ... This is the desire to be noticed by everyone! We live in a "selfie" culture. *"Look at me!"* is the motto of the social media movement. We are so easily excited by every "like" or flattering comment, yet remain unsatisfied. Being "noticed" and celebrated in this way is to ignore our higher calling—to glorify the Lord Jesus Christ! Can we find satisfaction?

The Satisfaction of a Father ... Colossians 1:19-23 – A soul is satisfied when it is in a right relationship with its Creator! No longer a stranger, an enemy, or an assailant—but now a son! We have a home and a purpose in our Father.

The Satisfaction of Fulfillment ... Colossians 1:19, 2:9-10 – The Lord is the only One able to fill the void of satisfaction because He fills our life to overflowing and satisfies the *true* hunger of our soul. (Psalm 23:5; Matthew 5:6)

The Satisfaction of Faith ... Colossians 1:23 – Faith feeds the soul because it gives purpose, peace, direction, and meaning! To walk by faith is to surrender control and be satisfied with Christ's Lordship over our lives. (Romans 10:9)

WALK IN VICTORY ... *Where have you been searching for soul satisfaction? Meditate on these "satisfaction" verses today: Psalm 16:11, 17:15, 90:14, 103:5, 107:9*

VICTORY!

DAVID'S RESOLUTIONS FOR LEADERS

"I will set nothing wicked before my eyes; I hate the work of those who fall away; It shall not cling to me. A perverse heart shall depart from me; I will not know wickedness."

PSALM 101:3-4

A leader, by definition, is someone who influences people for a clearly defined cause or goal. The difference between *good* leaders and *bad* leaders is the worthwhile nature of their cause or goal and their ability to motivate followers to join them!

It is my conclusion that God has called *every* Christian to be a leader. The world believes a leader is the person being served, but Christ said the complete opposite! "And whoever of you desires to be first shall be slave of all. For even the Son of Man did not come to be served, but to serve, and to give His life a ransom for many." (Mark 10:44-45) Every Christian is called to be a servant, and thus, called to be a leader! In Psalm 101, King David (one of history's greatest leaders) lays out several resolutions for leadership.

A strong leader must be a resolute servant. Throughout the Psalm, David says "I WILL." Is this pride? Often when you see "I will" repeated in the Bible, it is a red flag of self-reliance and a declaration of independence from God. Not here! David is declaring his absolute loyalty to God! This is an attitude of worship! David knows a *stronger* Leader when he sees One! No matter the circumstances, David was resolved to follow God as *his* leader. This is the only way to develop a true "I will" resolve. This proper perspective is developed when we remember Who is *really* in control! (v.1)

Strong leaders display spiritual discernment and integrity. (v.2) Wisdom is the ability to know God's Word and put it into practice. When applied, God's Word develops discernment and builds a life of integrity. David wants to build a life that desires God's presence, not a life that is consumed with impressing others. He desires to walk in wisdom rather than performance. Integrity is a genuine walk with the Lord. It means you are the same God-fearing, Christ-honoring person in every situation.

Godly discipline is another marker of strong leaders. The willingness to discern or evaluate everything that comes into your life. Jesus called this a "good eye" in Matthew 6:22-23. "The lamp of the body is the eye. If therefore your eye is good, your whole body will be full of light…" Jesus is talking about a focused, disciplined life. This kind of resolve shows singular focus, and a refusal to be sidetracked.

A strong leader is also self-controlled. (v.4) Departing from a "perverse heart" means you do not surrender control to impulses of anger or acts of violence. Not only does he determine to avoid this kind of attitude, but he even avoids the kind of people who live or speak in a "perverse" way or will he be guilty by association. (v.5)

Finally, strong leaders stand for what is right. (vv.6-8) David is determined to make a stand for righteousness and denounce sinful habits. Verses 4-5 and 7-8 all outline the enemies of a strong leader. A strong leader cannot practice such things if he desires to stand for righteousness. David knows he cannot pursue righteousness on his own, so he surrounds himself with good, strong companions to help. (v.6) We should resolve to do the same!

WALK IN VICTORY ... *David was not a perfect leader. Some of his greatest mistakes are well-documented in the Bible. As you humbly consider some of his failures from scripture (1 Corinthians 10:12), which of the leadership resolutions from Psalm 101 did he fail to remember? Should this discourage us from resolute living? Why or why not?*

STUCK TO THE SWORD

"[Eleazar] arose and attacked the Philistines until his hand was weary, and his hand stuck to the sword. The Lord brought about a great victory that day..."

2 SAMUEL 23:9-10

Eleazar, one of King David's "Mighty Men," leaves a lasting impression on the pages of scripture with only two verses to his name! While there are many fantastic stories in 2 Samuel 23, I believe this story of Eleazar illustrates a dynamic distinctive of Christian conduct in the midst of spiritual warfare.

DEVOTED SERVICE ... (v.9a) Eleazar was fully devoted to his king. If you desire to be a devoted servant of King Jesus, you must know His goals, direction, and mindset. The King's enemies must become your enemies, and you must grow to love the King's allies. As a servant of King Jesus, you must be completely devoted to knowing Him more, so as you grow to know Him more, you will think and act like Him. (1 Corinthians 2:16; Philippians 2:5)

DETERMINED STANCE ... (vv.9b-10a) When the men of Israel retreated, Eleazar "arose and attacked." Eleazar was determined to stand and fight! He would *not* give in to the enemy—even when everyone else was in full retreat! The boldness to stand and fight comes from knowing and living the Word of God! You cannot stand strong apart from His Spirit, and the Spirit's sword is God's Word! (Ephesians 6:17) Your enemy is spiritual, and so are your weapons! (2 Corinthians 10:4-6) Trying to stand in human wisdom is futile. (1 Corinthians 2:5)

DISCIPLINED SWORDSMAN ... (v.10b) Eleazar attacked the Philistines until his weary hand "stuck to the sword." This is wild! Eleazar's hand and his sword could not be separated—one was an extension of the other. What a testimony it would be if the Word of God could not be separated from the way we think and live! Is your life an inseparable extension of God's Word?

DELEGATED SUCCESS ... (v.10c) "The Lord brought about a great victory that day, and the people returned after him only to plunder." When the battle is won, the Lord gets the glory and others are blessed! As God blessed Eleazar with success, Eleazar blessed the returning combatants with the spoils of God's delegated success! Eleazar's willingness to stand strong in the battle encouraged others to return to the battlefield. Don't be soured by retreating soldiers reaping rewards! Be thankful for the victory won by the Lord and the fact that His army rallied behind bold leadership. Which kind of soldier are you? Which kind of solder do you want to be?

WALK IN VICTORY ... *Is your life an inseparable extension of God's Word?*

ENTHUSIASM THAT LASTS!

"These who have turned the world upside down have come here too."

ACTS 17:6

Christians should be the most enthusiastic people in the world!

Our English word "enthusiasm" comes from the Greek word *entheos* which has a pretty surprising origin! The first use of *entheos* was an attempt to describe the supernatural events happening during the time of the early Christian church. The unbelieving world did not have an explanation for the passionate fervor overflowing from the early church believers who had received the gift of the indwelling Holy Spirit. (Acts 2:2-8) Finding every adjective inadequate for these over-zealous Jesus-people, they opted for a combination of words to define their excessive religious zeal: *"en"* (meaning "in") and *"theos"* (meaning "God") formed the new derogatory insult *entheos*. This means, in its earliest iteration, "enthusiasm" was a sarcastic label for the "religious nuts" who were "possessed" by their God. Little did they know how right they were!

Over 2,000 years later, the zeal of the newborn church stings the deficiencies of our modern faith. The fact that the indwelling Holy Spirit produced such a strong reaction in the hearts and minds of *unbelievers* is both convicting *and* hopeful! The temptation is to either wallow in our lack of enthusiasm or attempt to "drum up" some over-hyped sense of emotionalism (which is not the same as authentic enthusiasm). However, the real answer is much simpler than that – be filled with the Holy Spirit! Think about it. We have the *same* indwelling Holy Spirit! We have the *same* message to be excited about – the Gospel of our Lord Jesus Christ! We are *IN GOD* and He is *IN US!* Our walk with the Lord (and everything else we do in life) should overflow with enthusiasm! We are the most excited, joy-filled, enthusiastic people because our power extends beyond our abilities; our joy does not depend on our circumstances; and our fears are crippled by the endurance of our message!

So today, give everyone you meet the *ENTHUSIASM THAT LASTS!*

WALK IN VICTORY *... What are you enthusiastic about in your life? Is your walk with God enthusiastic or apathetic? If your walk with God lacks enthusiasm today, how do you change? (See Galatians 5:16-17)*

DECLARING A VICTORIOUS GOSPEL

"Moreover, brethren, I declare to you the gospel which I preached to you, which also you received and in which you stand."

1 CORINTHIANS 15:1

Before Paul thanks God for the victory we have in our Lord Jesus Christ (1 Corinthians 15:57), he "declares" the victorious Gospel he once "preached." How are these things different? The way I see it, Paul preached the Gospel verbally, but declared the victory of the Gospel through a radically changed life! Paul was big on lifestyle observation (see 1 Corinthians 11:1), so let's look at Paul as an example of declaring a victorious Gospel with your life.

Paul Declared a Changed Life – "For I delivered to you first of all that which I also received: that Christ died for our sins according to the Scriptures, and that He was buried, and that He rose again the third day according to the Scriptures." (1 Corinthians 15:3-4) Can you believe it? Here we see the once notorious anti-Jesus, Christian hunter called Saul of Tarsus declaring the death, burial, resurrection, and Messianic identity of Jesus of Nazareth. Wow! What a changed life! This drastic change is the same one we experience in Christ. We might not have Paul's dramatic story, but we do have the Christ-life! That is the *real* testimony—not who we *were*, but Who we *are* in Christ by His grace! (15:9-11)

Paul Declared a Crucified Life – By the grace of God, Paul declared a crucified life. Paul remembers who he once was and recognizes who he now is. But as Paul continues to preach and declare the Gospel, he often reminds followers of Christ that we now live a crucified life. "It is no longer I who live, but Christ lives in me..." (Galatians 2:20) We are powerless to live the Christ-life on our own, and our flesh continues to declare war against every effort to walk with the Lord. But we are not alone! It is the Lord Jesus Christ Who gives us the victory over sin, Satan, and the world system to declare a victorious Gospel through a crucified life! (1 Corinthians 15:57)

Paul Declared a Consecrated Life – Paul's changed, crucified life was now set apart for Christ's service. This new life was manifested on a path of holiness. Paul was now a holy person with a holy purpose living out God's holy plan. Again, this path of holy living does not belong exclusively to Paul. Through the victorious Gospel, this life is ours too!

WALK IN VICTORY ... *Has your life been changed, crucified, and consecrated through the victorious Gospel? Can others see and imitate it? (1 Corinthians 11:1)*

RENEWED LIKE THE EAGLE – PART 1

"Who satisfies your mouth with good things..."

PSALM 103:5

Every Camp Eagle alum knows this one by heart! It is the declaration enthusiastically raised before every meal: "Who satisfies your mouth with good things so that your youth is renewed like the eagle's." This is far more than a pre-meal tradition—it is a deep truth to be lived!

Eagles endure a methodical, almost year-round process of molting and preening feathers to ensure, with fresh plumage, the wear and tear of the previous year dissolves into a "renewed" appearance of youth and vigor. The scripture's command to "be new" is impossible on our own. No amount of positive thinking or self-motivated *"pull myself up by my bootstraps"* can take something old and make it brand new.

So how does it happen? Here are a few noteworthy points from the first half of this verse:

"Who satisfies" ... Only God can satisfy. This is both a challenging reminder and a blessed assurance. By way of reminder, the Good Shepherd would have us recall the times when we have sought out "greener grass" in the pastureland of sinful indulgence, only to find this "satisfaction" to be temporary and sour. Nevertheless, that same Good Shepherd confidently assures us, "The LORD is my shepherd; I shall not want. He makes me lie down in green pastures; He leads me beside the still waters." (Psalm 23:1-2)

"your mouth" ... God meets our needs. In this case, "Who satisfies *your mouth*" refers to a need that is basic, but essential. The needs of our mouth are not glamorous but left unattended and unsatisfied, they can kill us. Food, drink, and oxygen – the three most basic needs of physical life – are satisfactions met through the mouth. Furthermore, God assures us that He (the "*Who*") will be the One Who satisfies our mouths with "good things."

"with good things" ... God gives us *what* we need *when* we need it. True satisfaction cannot be found in anything temporary. True satisfaction can only come from "*good* things." How? Because everything truly good is from God! (Romans 8:28; James 2:17) Every "good" thing is fully supplied in the Lord Jesus Christ! (Philippians 4:19) Anything that truly satisfies will have God's goodness in it because God has hardwired our hearts for Himself.

WALK IN VICTORY ... *Are you trusting or doubting God's "good things" today?*

RENEWED LIKE THE EAGLE – PART 2

"… so that your youth is renewed like the eagle's."

PSALM 103:5

Yesterday we talked about the conditions leading up to the process of "renewal." Today, we want to answer a simple question: *"Why do I need to be renewed?"*

As mentioned yesterday, eagles endure a methodical, almost year-round process of preening and molting their feathers to eliminate the wear and tear of the previous year for a "renewed" appearance. In simplest terms, "preening" is the feather maintenance routine for removing dirt, eliminating parasites, waterproofing, and properly aligning feathers for flying and diving. "Molting" is the gradual process of replacing feathers that are too old or damaged to preen back into shape. These two meticulous, ongoing processes work harmoniously to help the eagle be "renewed" as the old is systematically eliminated to make room for the new! As a believer, the process of old things passing away to make room for all things becoming new begins to resemble the renewal process of the eagle in Psalm 103:5!

PREENING … An eagle spends almost as much time cleaning and aligning its wings for flight as it does in the air. Why? Because feathers are delicate, precise instruments and need to be in near-perfect condition for optimal flight. Unfortunately, many Christians will spend much of their life attempting to fly a faith that is not aligned with the Gospel. Preening also removes health-compromising dirt and parasites. Are we submitting to the Holy Spirit for the removal of parasitic fears and the dirt of sin? Renewal demands realignment to the holiness of God! (2 Corinthians 5:17)

MOLTING … A renewed eagle will eliminate any feathers hindering optimal flight. In other words, the eagle identifies the dead weight that could potentially kill him! When Jesus died for our sins, He crucified our flesh (the "old man") on the cross. (Romans 6:6) The Holy Spirit is a testimony of the death and burial of the old nature which would kill our faith and steal our joy! The Spirit is also a testimony of the renewed, youthful life we have in the Lord Jesus! Thanks be to God for the *VICTORY* we have in the Lord Jesus!

WALK IN VICTORY … *Are you wholly surrendered to Christ so the "new man" can grow and prosper? (2 Corinthians 5:17) Or are you still clinging to old, dead things that have passed away? (Romans 6:11-14)*

34

DO YOU WANT TO FOLLOW JESUS?

"Whoever wants to be My disciple must deny themselves and take up their cross daily and follow Me."

LUKE 9:23

Following Jesus as Lord and Savior is marked by the building blocks of commitment ("Jesus is my Lord") and trust ("Jesus is my Savior"). These, working in harmony, are what the Bible calls "faith." The Holy Spirit plants these desires in a new Christian like a tiny ember in a bed of coals—they just need to be fanned into flame! In Luke 9, Jesus is speaking to a group of would-be followers, and as we can see, the call to follow Jesus as "Lord and Savior" is not an easy one!

There is a decision to be made. "Whoever wants to be…" This is a commitment of the will. Your life will be surrendered and your trust will be transferred. This is truly a matter of life and death!

There is a new direction to be lived out. "…My disciple…" This is a definitive turn from sin to the Savior. We call this "repentance" (a change of mind, will, and direction). The decision (faith) and direction (repentance) cannot be separated! They go hand-in-hand.

There is a denial of "my way." Jesus continues, "…My disciple must deny themselves…" Genuine salvation is marked by a person who desires to please the Lord rather than himself. This is not optional! Notice the disciple *must* deny. This is not a passive request to live God's way, but an absolute requirement. (See 1 Corinthians 6:19-20)

There is a death to the old way of living. Followers of Jesus must "…take up their cross…" Christ's death on the cross was not glamorous or easy. It was cruel and hard and was the culmination of His suffering. But followers of Christ identify with the cross because we are prepared to suffer for His glory!

Finally, Jesus calls for faithful devotion. "… take up the cross *daily*, and follow Me…" Devotion to Christ means followers of Christ do not place their faith on the "back burner" of life and forget about it. This is a new identity! And every true believer has a genuine, ongoing desire to devote every aspect of his life to the Lord Jesus Christ.

WALK IN VICTORY … *Do you want to follow Jesus? (1) Realize you are a sinner who has offended a holy God. [Romans 3:23] (2) Recognize that Christ died on the cross to pay the debt for your sin. [Romans 6:23; 2 Corinthians 5:21] (3) Repent and turn away from your life of sin. [Acts 3:19] (4) Receive Christ as Lord and Savior! [Romans 10:9-11] (5) REJOICE! You are a born-again follower of Jesus! [Luke 15:1-7]*

DON'T BE AN "ALMOST"

Then Agrippa said to Paul, "You almost persuade me to become a Christian."

ACTS 26:28

The Buffalo Bills have the distinction of being the only NFL team to ever advance to four consecutive Super Bowls. They also have the unfortunate distinction of losing all four games—the four-time *ALMOST* champions! History is filled with countless "almost" situations. While most of these "almost" situations will not matter in light of eternity, that is not the case in Acts 26:28. "Then Agrippa said to Paul, 'You almost persuade me to become a Christian.'" Was this a sarcastic remark or a genuine moment? We don't know, but the consequence of being an "almost Christian" is a sad reality.

How many "almost Christians" sit in churches throughout the world every Sunday? Being an "almost" Super Bowl champion might put you in the history books, but being an "almost Christian" will not ink your name into the Lamb's Book of Life! To be "almost" saved from deep water is to drown. To be "almost" saved from a fire is to burn. You cannot be "almost" saved. You are either in or out, hot or cold, saved or unsaved. You will either spend an eternity with God, or an eternity without God—there is no middle ground!

But what about Christians? Is there an "almost" for us as well? Certainly! Psalm 73:1-3 says, "Truly God is good to Israel, to such as are pure in heart. But as for me, my feet had almost stumbled; My steps had nearly slipped. For I was envious of the boastful when I saw the prosperity of the wicked." Christian, you are just as near to a deadly "almost" today. When we look at the "success" of the world and become envious, we are on the verge of an "almost" backslide. What will help us refocus when we are on the verge of stumbling? Psalm 73:17-19 says, "Until I went into the sanctuary of God; Then I understood their end. Surely *You set them in slippery places; You cast them down to destruction.* Oh, how they are brought to desolation, as in a moment!" (emphasis added) God's powerful presence reminds us of the fate of the wicked. King Agrippa probably seemed like the more successful person that day in Acts 26, but like the wicked in Psalm 73, Agrippa's end was destruction while Paul's "end" was the presence of the Lord Jesus! (Philippians 1:21) "Almost" and "halfway" are not God's way! (See Revelation 3:15-16)

WALK IN VICTORY ... *Are you an "almost" Christian today? What is keeping you from repenting and believing the Good News about the Lord Jesus Christ right now? Christian: Are your eyes and heart distracted? Are you "almost" backsliding? Reset your focus on the Lord today!*

DO'S & DON'TS

"Not by works of righteousness which we have done, but according to His mercy He saved us, through the washing of regeneration and renewing of the Holy Spirit."

TITUS 3:5

Many times in our Christian walk we view our relationship with God as a bunch of "do's and don'ts." You better DO this! You better NOT do that! DO *this*; DON'T do *that*! This often becomes the way we define our relationship with God—performance review.

But is this what our walk with God is like? Is God really sitting on His throne waiting for us to mess up so He can instantly judge our failures and bop us on the head? Not at all!

Certainly, there are things we should and should not do as Christians, but these are motivated by scriptural understanding, spiritual maturity, and—most importantly—supernatural love. In other words, I *want* to DO the things that please God, and I *DON'T* want to do the things that displease Him. But the amazing thing is whether I DO or DON'T, it does not change my righteous standing before God!

Titus 3:3-8 discusses this truth. Works don't save us! God's abundant mercy (v.5) and grace (v.7) bring us into a right relationship with Himself, making us heirs of Christ's righteousness. While it is true we cannot do anything to earn God's favor, God's favor rests on His Son, Jesus! And since we have been given the life of the Lord Jesus, God's favor is freely given to us because of His Son! (Romans 4:5; Philippians 3:9; Ephesians 1:6)

Where do righteous works come in then? According to these verses, righteous works come *after* salvation, not before! They are the evidence of a life made right with God—the result of the Holy Spirit within. In this way, good works are the response of a heart of worship, not the prerequisite of a heart worth saving. They bring God glory and honor because without Him we can do nothing. (John 15:5) They are "good and profitable to men." (Titus 3:8) So even though works do not earn God's favor, they are the result of understanding and living in God's favor. This is the victorious Christian life! Determine to live in the victory of God's mercy and grace! He loves us through mercy and grace!

WALK IN VICTORY *… Are you basing your standing before God on a list of "do's and don'ts?" Remember your good works are an act of love from a thankful heart of worship. Thank God for His mercy and grace today!*

EYES FIXED ON NEED

"Then Peter said, 'Silver and gold I do not have, but what I do have I give you: In the name of Jesus Christ of Nazareth, rise up and walk.' And he took him by the right hand and lifted him up, and immediately his feet and ankle bones received strength."

ACTS 3:6-7

Acts 3 tells the amazing story of ministering to a man in tremendous need! As Peter and John went into the temple, Peter fixed his eyes on a man with an insurmountable need. The Lord then used Peter to do a mighty miracle which brought praise to God, met the physical need of the man, and gave witness to all who saw which opened an opportunity to share the Gospel with many people.

One of the great benefits of knowing Jesus Christ as our Lord and Savior is the opportunity to serve Him by serving others. A key to accomplishing ministry is having eyes fixed on the needs of people around us. Every day we come into contact with people who have physical, emotional, mental, and spiritual needs. Have you noticed? Or are you too wrapped up in routine and consumed by the needs of your own life?

Noticing the needs of others around you reflects your walk with the Lord— the One Who always had His eyes fixed on the needs of others! Peter and John were living in such a way that as soon as they saw the lame man, they immediately noticed and acted. By ministering to this man's physical needs, the door was opened to minister to his spiritual need and the spiritual needs of many others.

Our ministry to others must start with eyes fixed on need! Do you act when you notice the needs of others? By this, our Lord is glorified and the Gospel is made alive!

WALK IN VICTORY ... *To meet the needs of others, we must be willing to live generously. Are you living with a generous spirit today? (See Acts 2:44-45) Pray and ask the Lord to provide the opportunity, capacity, and generosity to meet a specific need today for the sake of the Gospel.*

THE CRUCIFIED LIFE

"I have been crucified with Christ; it is no longer I who live, but Christ lives in me; and the life which I now live in the flesh I live by faith in the Son of God, who loved me and gave Himself for me."

GALATIANS 2:20

I don't want to live a "normal" life. What about you? I want to see real, supernatural power in my life and ministry—the kind of power that Moses and the Israelites saw at the Red Sea. The power that slew a giant by the hands of a boy and gave Peter the ability to walk on water! *That* kind of power! I can guess what you are thinking. "Come on, man! That was in those old days. God doesn't do that today!" I disagree! I think that same power is alive and well in us today through the crucified life. You might say, "I don't want to live a crucified life! That sounds miserable and hard!" Okay, then—I believe you have revealed whether or not you want the power of God in your life. You see, I don't want to be crucified either, but God has to get plain old "me" out of the way so I can experience the power of the crucified life!

IDENTIFICATION ... "I am crucified with Christ" – When people look at your life, who do they see? Identifying with Christ's death is vitally important because this is where we acknowledge that He took our place. He is the sacrifice for our sin.

CRUCIFIXION ... "it is no longer I who live" – The old man (our dead, sinful nature) was crucified with Christ. In this way, we identify with the death and burial of Christ because the grave brings finality. That old man is *GONE!*

SANCTIFICATION ... "but Christ lives in me" – The "new man" is the consecrated temple of the Holy Spirit! We *are* holy and we are *being made* holy. "Christ lives IN ME!" What a promise! We are sealed by His Holy Spirit.

APPLICATION ... "and the life which I now live in the flesh" – Paul says in Romans 6:4 that we now "walk in newness of life." What does this entail? It means we have new desires, new focus, new life, new behavior, and new destination! How is all this possible? We live by faith! (Romans 1:17)

GLORIFICATION ... "I live by faith in the Son of God, Who loved me and gave Himself for me" – The crucified life is not some temporary fluke. This condition is permanent! Even better—this condition will one day be *perfected* when we are bodily resurrected in Christ! The crucified are citizens of heaven!

WALK IN VICTORY ... *Are you living the crucified life? Do you see its power at work in your life?*

VICTORY!

ENEMIES OF THE CRUCIFIED LIFE

"There were also two others, criminals, led with Him to be put to death. And when they had come to the place called Calvary, there they crucified Him, and the criminals, one on the right hand and the other on the left."

LUKE 23:32-33

There are three main enemies to the crucified life: self ("the flesh"), Satan ("the accuser"), and the system (that is, the world and its anti-God way of living). These three enemies pop up in several stories in the Bible. From the Garden of Eden to Christ's temptation in the wilderness and even at the scene of the crucifixion, these three adversaries always seem to be present at critical points in the story. Today, we will examine the last example to see how the enemies of the crucified life were present at the cross of Christ Himself. [Read Luke 23:32-46]

While the two thieves were suffering the same gruesome execution as Christ, their reactions to the situation are quite different. One reviles the Lord and says, "If You are the Christ, save Yourself and us." (v.39) This thief represents the self-life. "Save *Yourself*. Think about number one!" This is always how the flesh tempts us. But our Lord knew there was no way to accomplish both directives: "…save Yourself *and* us." No way. To save mankind, Christ could not be saved from His cross.

In a similar fashion to Satan's accusation and temptation in the wilderness, everyone wants Jesus to take a shortcut. "Abandon the cross, Jesus!" Whenever Satan accuses and tempts, he always wants the crucified Christian to abandon the cross and live the "easy life." Do NOT listen to his lies!

The religious leaders and Roman soldiers (representing the system of this world) also mocked Christ's cross with the same message of self-preservation. The religious leaders want Him to prove He is the Messiah. The soldiers want Christ to prove He is King. They wrongly think Christ could prove these identities through preservation, survival, and comfort, but the exact *opposite* is true! Isn't it interesting that all three enemies of the crucified life desire the same thing? "Save *Yourself*!" Enemies of the crucified life believe the life of a crucified Christian is crazy, but we know the truth. The only way to truly live is to die. (Galatians 2:20) And the greatest power on earth is self-sacrificial love. (1 John 4:7-12)

WALK IN VICTORY *… Are you seeking to live the crucified life or playing around with its enemies? (See 1 John 2:15-17)*

FREEDOM!

"For he who has died has been freed from sin."

ROMANS 6:7

During the American Civil War, a rich southern aristocrat hired a young man to go and fight on his behalf. The young man went to war using the name of the rich southern gentleman. (This would allow the rich man to get credit for fighting in the war without actually going! Can you believe it?) After several months of combat, the substitute was killed in battle, and a death certificate was sent to the aristocrat. To his surprise, he was now legally dead!

Several years later, the rich aristocrat was taken to court for dishonest gain and stealing. The prosecutor had ample evidence to convict, so there was no doubt he was guilty. But in the courtroom, as a defense, the rich man presented the death certificate stating he was legally dead! As a dead man, he could not be guilty of such crimes. After examining the death certificate, the judge declared the man "not guilty." The judge concluded that the certificate proved the man's death, so this "dead man" could not be convicted.

Thanks be to God through Christ's death we are free! Our identification with the cross of Christ has made us legally dead to sin, but alive to God! According to Romans 6:11, "Likewise, you also, reckon yourselves to be dead indeed to sin, but alive to God in Christ Jesus our Lord." In other words, do the math! If we have been given new life because of Christ's victory over sin on the love-motivated day, we are dead to trespasses and sins. No matter the offense, we will not be found guilty of sin because of what Christ has done in our place! Praise God!

But this identification does not give a Christian the license to practice sin! Unlike the rich man who abused his status to break the law, a Christian uses his new status to live in victorious freedom and serve God! (Romans 6:1) Paul summarizes both sides of this perfectly in Romans 8:1. "There is therefore now no condemnation to those who are in Christ Jesus, who do not walk according to the flesh, but according to the Spirit." There is a declaration of position: "There is therefore now no condemnation to those who are in Christ Jesus..." And a declaration of practice: "...who do not walk according to the flesh, but according to the Spirit." It is the position that makes the practice a reality! They go hand-in-hand. Christian, do not abandon your freedom by living again in the bonds of sin! You have been set free!

WALK IN VICTORY ... *Does your life (practice) reflect your freedom from sin (position)? Meditate on Romans 6:1-14 today.*

FOUR FUNDAMENTAL TRUTHS

"Therefore, whether you eat or drink, or whatever you do, do all to the glory of God."

1 CORINTHIANS 10:31

I believe that there are three main elements of being a good coach: the ability to teach, the ability to motivate confidence in a common goal, and the ability to know and communicate the fundamentals. Some might say the fundamentals are "no-brainers," but if we fail to review them, we will drift from them! When I read God's Word, I see four fundamental truths for effective life and ministry:

FUNDAMENTAL TRUTH #1
Our Motivating Purpose: GLORIFY GOD (1 Corinthians 10:31)

Our purpose in life and ministry is to GLORIFY GOD! To "glory" means to give the proper, weighty opinion of someone—in this case, God! Everything I do in life and ministry should give the right opinion of God. From the essential, mundane act of eating and drinking up to "whatever you do," we are supposed to give the right opinion of God to the watching world around us! God's power and presence must permeate every aspect of our lives!

FUNDAMENTAL TRUTH #2
Our Compelling Reality: HELL IS REAL (Revelation 20:11-15)

I must admit, this one burdens me greatly! I do not believe any Christian can be right with God and not be moved by the seriousness of this passage! The reality of God's just response to unrepentant sinners must drive us to action! This need isn't just across the globe—it's HERE! It's in your family, your neighborhood, and your city. If we are fundamentally here to glorify God, we must share His truth!

FUNDAMENTAL TRUTH #3
Our Reliable Method: THE WORD of GOD (Romans 1:16; Hebrews 4:12)

When I was first hired as Camp Director, I was given an assignment to write a 13-lesson curriculum explaining the Gospel from Genesis to Revelation. In 2000, we used it for the first time with about 65 campers. We prayed and trusted the Lord for a great harvest of souls! After walking all week through God's big story of Creation, The Fall, and Redemption, I gave the invitation on Thursday night. Out of 65 campers, almost two-thirds of the room stood up and began walking forward—I was shocked. I yelled, *"STOP!"* (I thought they misunderstood the invitation as a dismissal.) I explained the invitation again and warned them *not* to come forward unless they were serious about trusting Jesus as Lord and Savior. Again, 40+ campers stood up and walked forward. I wept. Friends, God's Word is *POWERFUL* and *RELIABLE* to change lives!

FUNDAMENTAL TRUTH #4
Our Trustworthy Confidence: THE LORD JESUS CHRIST (1 John 5:11-15)

We *only* have LIFE in the Lord Jesus Christ! This life is evident when we walk by the Spirit. Galatians 5:16 says, "I say then: Walk in the Spirit, and you shall not fulfill the lust of the flesh." Living in Christ's life means denying the self-life. Through faith in Christ, we have confidence, boldness, and access to God. "He hears us"—we read this statement two times! (5:14 and 5:15) Prayer is the evidence that you find your confidence in the Lord! Lack of prayer is evidence of self-confidence, not God-centered reliance. Prayer is a foundational piece of the Christian life because prayer is communion with Life Himself!

WALK IN VICTORY ... *Have you forgotten any of the fundamentals of your faith? Consider searching the Scripture to develop your own personal "fundamentals" or "pillars" of life and ministry.*

GO INTO THE UNREAL WORLD AND BE REAL!

"Simon Peter said to them, 'I am going fishing' ... and that night they caught nothing."

JOHN 21:3

At the end of every week of camp, I challenge our camp staff with the same message before they head home for the weekend: "Go into the *unreal* world and *BE REAL!*" You might say, *"Come on, man! Camp ministry is an unreal world! No phones or internet? Get real!"*

"Get real." I like that! That's good advice for a Christian in the Lord's army! Live in the *REAL* world! I would argue that there is nothing more real than living life for the Lord Jesus Christ! "I am *the way, the truth*, and *the life*. No one comes to the Father except *through Me*." (John 14:6, emphasis added) Is there anything more real than that? The *unreal* world, filled with bondage and distractions, thinks living for the things of God can't be real life. *"You need to grow up and grow out of that stuff!"* But outgrowing a clearly defined Way, Truth, and Life is exactly how we ended up in this unreal mess! No, we cannot go back to the unreal world unless we bring Christ's reality with us!

This reminds me of the story in John 21 when Peter and six other disciples return to the unreal world. Was Peter bored, broke, or bound to his former profession? We don't know. But after a fruitless night of fishing, the Lord appears to His disciples and redirects their fishing to a miraculous haul! Instantly, Peter and John realize Who is on shore, so Peter dives overboard and swims to the beach. (vv.4-8) After breakfast on the beach, Christ's threefold commission to lovingly lead God's flock reinstates Peter (vv.15-17) who was probably still reeling from his trio of denials in John 18.

We often go back to the unreal world when we are reeling because it is a recognizable world. Jesus did not scold the disciples for fishing—He simply showed them that He had bigger, more "real world" plans for their lives if they would follow His lead. (vv. 5-6, 15-22) Like Peter, we need to leap out of the comfort of the known, *unreal* world and return to the source of the real world—the Lord Jesus Christ! Once we have left the unreal world through salvation in Christ, we no longer feel "at home" there. The unreal will never satisfy the real hunger of the soul! Have you drifted back into the unreal world? The Lord Jesus has an abundant "real world" plan for your life!

WALK IN VICTORY ... In moments of uncertainty, do you "go back" to what you know in the unreal world? Check out these "no going back" scriptures: Galatians 5:1; Proverbs 26:11; Philippians 3:13-15; Luke 9:57-62

HIGH STAKES

"Awake to righteousness, and do not sin; for some do not have the knowledge of God. I speak this to your shame."

1 CORINTHIANS 15:34

This chapter is a logically flowing, deeply significant doctrinal discourse until Paul interrupts himself with a quick point of application in verses 33 and 34. I want us to look at verse 34 in particular to see our responsibility in the "high stakes" commitment of walking with God.

WAKE UP! ... "Awake to righteousness..." In other words, don't walk around in a spiritual stupor! We need to open our eyes to the plight of the unreal world because people are dying and heading into a Christless eternity! The command to "awake" means to be alert or keenly aware of our spiritual surroundings. Do not fall asleep on duty, soldier of the cross! Do you see things in the light of eternity, or are you walking around in a spiritual stupor?

WALK UP! ... "Awake to righteousness, and do not sin..." The New Testament often refers to our manner of life as a "walk." Modern Christianity seems to be satisfied with an abundance of "low walking." God has called each Christian to live like a child of the king! (1 Peter 2:9-10) This is a high calling! Cast off the mundane and embrace the marvelous!

WISE UP! ... "for some do not have the knowledge of God..." Each one of us is responsible for the gifts God has given us—including the gift of knowing God! We are usually fearless in sharing what we know, but seem to be shy about sharing the knowledge of God! The problem is obvious, right? The stakes are too high to be timid about sharing the Lord Jesus Christ!

WEEP UP! ... "I speak this to your shame." The world sins shamelessly. Unfortunately, too many Christians have adopted this policy as well! Do we not care that living in sin shames the name of Christ? We need to realize the broken condition of our witness and mourn! Too many Christians are trying to be "cool" instead of holy, and the only mention of being "cool" in the Bible is negative! (Revelation 3:15-16) Christian, do not bring shame and reproach to your heavenly Father! (Mark 8:38) When you pass from this side of eternity to the next, what will people say about your relationship with God?

WALK IN VICTORY ... *Are you "low walking" in the ways of the world or "high walking" according to the standards of God? The stakes are high! The lost world is watching and looking for LIFE!*

45

HOW TO BE A WEAK-KNEED, SPINELESS, COMPROMISING WIMP

"And the Philistine said, 'I defy the armies of Israel this day; give me a man, that we may fight together.' When Saul and all Israel heard these words of the Philistine, they were dismayed and greatly afraid."

1 SAMUEL 17:10-11

The story of David and Goliath is one of the most well-known stories in all of the Bible! Often, the story focuses on Goliath's immense size, David's incredible faith, and the final resting place of a smooth stone hurled from a sling. But today, I want us to learn from the "other guys" in the story—the Israelite army.

These soldiers were weak-kneed. (v.11) They failed to stand firm when faced with opposition. They were called out! And even worse, their GOD was called out! Yet they had no desire to fight back. A weak-kneed Christian will follow their example in this way: (1) Fail to Stand on God's Person. (vv. 37, 45-47) In other words, think that God is small and incapable! That will definitely give you "weak knees." (2) Fail to Stand on God's Promises. (Deuteronomy 7:2) If you want weak knees, make you doubt anything God says He will do! (3) Fail to Stand on Prayer. (Psalm 18:3, 86:7) When the enemy attacks, your first response (unless you want weak knees) should be crying out to God in prayer!

Israel's army was also spineless! (v.24) Without a backbone, your entire body would collapse! Spineless Christians are forgetful. They buckle under the weight of every fear and doubt. How do we avoid this? (1) Remember your position in God. (Ephesians 1:6) You are completely accepted in Christ and treasured by God! (2) Remember your provision in God. (2 Peter 1:3) God has given you everything you need to live the Christ-life. You are an overcomer in Christ! (3) Remember your purpose in God. (1 Corinthians 10:31) You were made to glorify God in all things! He is able and willing to empower you to do so! (4) Remember your protection in God. (Romans 8:35-39) God's greatest promise is His powerful, loving presence! This is not a means to avoid hardship, but the power to endure hardship.

King Saul's army was full of compromisers! (vv.11, 24-25, 38-39) Compromisers yield to their enemy in the face of opposition. Their only goal is an easy win, not a worthwhile cause. They only fight if they know they will win! There is no sacrifice, only safety. A compromiser allows the enemy to take control of the situation, which is slavery. (Romans 6:16) The children of Israel compromised to Goliath's looks, lies, and laughter—which meant that one day, the Philistines would become their lords. (v.9)

Finally, these guys were wimps! (v.28) A wimp is someone who refuses to take responsibility or lead in the face of danger. A wimp embodies all of the characteristics listed above. This person is not only afraid but is also jealous of anyone who is willing to take a stand or be faithful. A wimpy Christian will discredit, discourage, and disagree with faith-filled Christians. He is deceived and wants others to be deceived as well. Don't be a weak-kneed, spineless, compromising wimp, Christian!

WALK IN VICTORY ... *Read 1 Samuel 17—what new details stood out to you as you read? Remember, Christian, the victory is already won in Christ Jesus our Lord!*

If you want a practical example of "living in light of victory," check out how Israel's army lived in light of a defeated foe! (See verses 51-54)

STANDING IN AN EVIL DAY

"Therefore, take up the whole armor of God, that you may be able to withstand in the evil day, and having done all, to stand."

EPHESIANS 6:13

While Ephesians 5 deals with how we should walk alongside others as a reflection of our walk with God, chapter 6 is a declaration of war! We stand against the spiritual powers that oppose our effective walk with God and man. (6:11,13a,13b) The link between walking well and standing firm is the setting—an evil day. (see 5:15-16; 6:13) *Despite* the evil day, we walk by faith! *Because* of the evil day, we stand firm in the faith! How do we do it?

STAND in COURAGE … There is no room for cowards in the evil day! The enemy assault is upon us! How can we be courageous? (1) Know the truth! (2) Side with truth! (Romans 8:28-31) Will you live an unashamed life of courage? (Joshua 1:6,9)

STAND in TRUTH … Truth is the only thing that sets us free from the bondage of sin! (John 8:32) There is no foundation without truth. Lies will always be washed away when trouble comes. The truth will stand! Dig in and stand firm on the rock of Christ! (Matthew 7:24-27)

STAND without COMPROMISE … Satan loves to undermine God's truth. Remember his first big lie in Genesis 3? *"Did God really say…?"* Our enemy wants us to live in doubt instead of confidence because doubt opens the door to compromise! Compromise wants to add to or subtract from the truth of God to make it "fit" with the world's way of thinking and living. Stand firm with uncompromising confidence in the Lord!

WALK in POWER … The Gospel is the power of God! (Romans 1:16) Do you want to walk through the evil day with great power? Know the Jesus Christ as Lord and Savior! *LIVE* like He is your *LORD* and *SAVIOR!*

WALK in BOLDNESS … A.W. Tozer once said, "Christians should be the boldest people in the world—not cocky and sure of ourselves, but sure of Him." Boldness is the willingness to stand on God's truth and walk in God's love. When we have both truth and love, we can stand with great boldness—even if we stand alone.

WALK by FAITH … Someone once said, "You might be the only Jesus someone ever meets." If that is true, then our lives better look like His! If we desire to live like the Lord, we must walk by faith! (Hebrews 11:6)

VICTORY!

WALK in VICTORY ... We are on the winning side! We are often tempted to feel defeated or discouraged by our failures, but we know that *our* spiritual performance does not earn the victory! The Lord Jesus earned our victory through His cross and resurrection, so we are now free to stand and walk confidently in an evil day through His victory! (1 Corinthians 15:57)

WALK in YOUR DAY ... Friend, you have been called by God to walk through life in this evil day. You are here for a purpose—to serve and please the Lord Jesus Christ! Do not waste your time wishing you had someone else's life! Redeem *your day* and *your time* where the Lord has placed you. (Ephesians 5:16)

WALK IN VICTORY ... *Have you identified the true enemies in the evil day? (see 6:10-13) Are you standing firm against these enemies or giving in to their lies?*

IS CHURCH ATTENDANCE NECESSARY?

"For the equipping of the saints for the work of ministry, for the edifying of the body of Christ, till we all come to the unity of the faith and of the knowledge of the Son of God..."

EPHESIANS 4:12-13

Falling into the bad habit of skipping church is an unhealthy practice. Not only do we miss out on the encouragement of gathering, but we also miss out on the opportunity to love and serve one another! The Lord desires to use His body of believers (the church) as a tool for transformation. But is attendance necessary? Can I just *be* the church and not *attend* any one church?

Necessary for Exercising our Spiritual Gifts ... "And He Himself gave some to be apostles, some prophets, some evangelists, and some pastors and teachers..." (4:11) God's indwelling Holy Spirit empowers us with "gifts" to encourage one another! These gifts are designed to shape each other into the image of Christ and model the fullness of Christ's love and grace to one another.

Necessary for Equipping the Saints ... "For the equipping of the saints..." (v.12) Saints (that is, all believers) are equipped as ministers. We gather to enhance this equipping for public ministry as well as practice our equipping through church ministry. In this way, we gather with the goal of spiritual maturity.

Necessary for Encouraging through Service ... "for the work of the ministry..." (v.12) One of the church's main tasks is to encourage one another to serve. We have the example of the Lord Jesus Who perfectly modeled a servant's heart. We must live a life of surrender to serve like Christ. (see John 13:1-17)

Necessary for Edifying the Saints ... "for the edifying of the body of Christ, till we all come to the unity of the faith and of the knowledge of the Son of God..." (vv.12-13) This word edify means to "to build up as in architecture." One of the main reasons we come together as a church is to encourage ("build up") one another! To live like Christ is not easy, and this old world will do everything it can to discourage us. Who is supposed to encourage us in the Christ-life? It must be those who have the life of Christ within!

Necessary for Evolving into the Stature of Christ's Fullness ... "to a perfect man, to the measure of the stature of the fullness of Christ..." (v.13) According to this verse, God's architectural plans for "building up" every believer will lead us to look like Christ! As we gather, the church exercises, equips, encourages, and edifies until we are *fully* like Christ.

WALK IN VICTORY ... *As you examine these five reasons for gathering, do they reflect the reason you choose to attend or skip? Or are your reasons for gathering more based on convenience, feelings, and preferences?*

LIKE A DIRTY SHIRT

"Now when He had said these things, He cried with a loud voice, 'Lazarus, come forth!' And he who had died came out bound hand and foot with graveclothes, and his face was wrapped with a cloth. Jesus said to them, 'Loose him, and let him go.'"

JOHN 11:43-44

As a little boy, it seemed that my siblings and I were often doing something mischievous and getting into trouble. My Father had a saying that he used to warn us of impending consequences for our actions. He would say, "I'm going to get all over you like a dirty shirt!" You might think this saying sounds funny or unusual, but when my dad said it, we knew that we had better change our behavior!

If you have ever worn an extremely dirty shirt, you know that it is uncomfortable, binding, and smelly (to say the least). It just makes you feel dirty! The filthy grave clothes of sin similarly bind us. In the account of Jesus raising Lazarus from the dead in John 11, the final instructions given by Jesus were, "Loose (unbind) him, and let him go!" While Jesus was only talking about physical grave clothes in this setting, the power of that resurrection statement goes much deeper!

When a sinner receives Jesus Christ as Lord and Savior, he is freed from the grave clothes of sin! As his regenerated soul stumbles out of its grave of sin, it hears the same command from the Son of God— "Unbind him, and let him go!" A child of God is no longer clothed in sin. No longer bound by stinking, sin-rotted rags from the grave. He is clothed in the righteousness of Jesus Christ!

So what does this mean? Christian, you no longer have to live in the binding, uncomfortable, stench of sin! Christ has set us free with His resurrection power! "Therefore, if anyone is in Christ, he is a new creation; old things have passed away; behold, all things have become new." (2 Corinthians 5:17) As a brand-new creation in Christ, you are free to live like Jesus! You have become a new you! If Christ has removed your sin like an old, dirty shirt, why would you put it back on again? Romans 6:2 asks, "How shall we who died to sin live any longer in it?" In other words, a shirt that dirty doesn't ever need to be worn again! Throw it out with the "old you" and live in victory today!

WALK IN VICTORY ... *Have you been set free from the bondage of sin? If so, do not yield to sin and put it back on like a dirty shirt! Take time to confess any known sin.*

LIVING IN ABUNDANCE

"I have come that they may have life, and that they may have it more abundantly."

JOHN 10:10

It is not surprising when the world gives Christianity a bad rap. They have no desire to live for Christ! (John 15:18-23) My trouble is not necessarily with the attack of the world—my issue is with the *Christians* who give Christianity a bad rap by living a life that makes Christianity not worth living! We cannot keep blaming the world for the negative views of Christianity. We must examine our walk with the Lord! In the first half of John 10:10, Jesus states the goal of the enemy this way: "The thief does not come except to steal, and to kill, and to destroy." I am tired of the enemy stealing our joy, killing our love, and destroying our witness! How can we change this? I want to live a life that clearly communicates, *"Christianity is a life worth living!"* I believe it starts with remembering that God has provided a "life worth living" in the Lord Jesus Christ! Let's look at the second half of John 10:10.

"I have come that they may have life, and that they may have it more abundantly." (John 10:10b) What is abundance? To have an "abundance" of something is to have more than you need. What an awesome truth! Christ has given us more than we need through His great grace! Notice the contrasting goals in John 10:10. Christ gives where the enemy steals. The Lord Who owns all things has the right to give all things! He holds nothing back because His generosity reflects His immense riches! (Psalm 50:10-12) Stealing reflects want and selfishness. Satan has nothing to give, he can only take. His strategy is to oppose Who God is and what God does. In the same vein, Christ gives life where Satan seeks to kill. And this is not just any life— Christ gives us *HIS* life! This life is above and beyond our comprehension! Christ's eternal life is active and alive in us right here, right now! Can you believe it? How could we ever ask, "Is this a life worth living?" *ABSOLUTELY!* Living in abundance is the opposite of Satan's goal of destruction; it is holy construction (or "edification") through the Christ-life!

Christ's abundance is manifested to us through His generosity! Living in abundance means Christ has given us: a new identity (Romans 6:5-10), an unfading inheritance (1 Peter 1:3-4), eternal security (John 10:28-29), protection (Romans 8:38-39), purposeful direction (Psalm 37:23), fulfillment (Psalm 16:11), peace (John 14:27), fellowship with God (John 15:12-17), God's tender care (1 Peter 5:7), and whatever else we need! (Philippians 4:19) Is this a life worth living? Yes—now and forevermore!

WALK IN VICTORY ... *Review the "gifts of abundance" passages listed above.*

LOVING GOD WITH ALL OF ME

"And you shall love the Lord your God with all your heart, with all your soul, with all your mind, and with all your strength. This is the first commandment."

MARK 12:30

I have met many atheists who claim to be good people—even deeply moral people! I am sure, by the world's standards, they are correct. But there is at least one moral ethic (in fact, the *greatest* moral ethic), that no atheist can keep. "Hear, O Israel: The LORD our God, the LORD is one. Love the LORD your God with all your heart and with all your soul and with all your strength" (Deuteronomy 6:4–5). This is known as the "Shema." The Jews would recite this declaration of loyalty every morning and evening as a sacred duty. The Lord Jesus cited the Shema as the "greatest commandment in the Law." (Matthew 22:36–37) Loving God with *ALL* of me is no small task! There is no greater evidence of man's inability to be "moral" on his own. Our fallen, sinful nature cannot possibly love as God commands, so how do I practically love God with *ALL* of me as a new man in Christ?

HEART ... God must be the focus of your affections. This is not emotional manipulation. Affections are developed with time and thought. Developing your heart-love for God means investing time and thought in His Word and prayer. Spending time in God's presence will reveal His great worth! Do you take pleasure in His ultimate worth?

SOUL ... God must be the central figure of your being. Worship reflects your genuine inner desires and intentions. To love God with all of your soul means that you are willing to dedicate every intention of your life. He becomes the "main character" in the story of your life.

MIND ... "Mind" did not appear in the original Shema prayer, but was added as the Christian faith was influenced by Greek culture. The mind was central in Greek philosophy, and the New Testament writers wanted their readers to know that God desires to be loved through your thinking too. Commitment to God isn't just feeling—it is also thinking as you train your intellect to align with His way of thinking.

STRENGTH ... God cares about your body. (Otherwise, He wouldn't resurrect it, right?) You must strive to serve God physically! Paul writes, "For we must all appear before the judgment seat of Christ, that each one may receive the *things done in the body,* according to what he has done, whether good or bad." (2 Corinthians 5:10, emphasis added) Devoting all your material capabilities to Him acknowledges His Lordship over your body.

WALK IN VICTORY ... *Which of these four aspects of loving God is most difficult?*

MIND-ALTERING LIVING: PURPOSE

"Jesus said to them, 'My food is to do the will of Him Who sent Me, and to finish His work.'"

JOHN 4:34

We know we understand the mind of Christ when we refuse to waste time. Every moment of life brims with *purpose*! When we waste time, it reveals an undisciplined life – a life that has yet to fully grasp the eternal purpose of the Christian life. "My food is to do the will of Him Who sent Me, and to finish His work." (John 4:34)

Jesus' declaration to the disciples reveals His eternal purpose and willingness to do whatever it takes to finish the job. We see this in the cross! Jesus humbly spent every drop of blood in an agonizing death because the will of the Father demanded a finished work. (Phil. 2:5-8; Matt. 26:52-54; John 19:30) Purpose and discipline are married in the will of the Father because His work is eternal and supernatural – in other words, it is not easy. Even though the will of the Father is not easy, it is our necessary food as disciples of Christ! Because the finished work of Jesus endures, our purpose within the Father's will nourishes us as it disciplines us to put to death the desires of the flesh. "No one can serve two masters [*conflicting purposes*]…" (Matthew 6:24a) God wants to institute mind-altering living in us, but we must be willing participants. By faith, we must discipline our energies to reflect the mind of Christ (Who was willing to endure anything to complete His purpose).

Paul said, "Therefore I run thus: not with uncertainty. Thus I fight: not as one who beats the air. But I discipline my body and bring it into subjection, lest, when I preach to others, I myself should become disqualified." (1 Corinthians 9:26-27)

Run with certainty. Fight actual opponents. Pursue real purpose. A lack of discipline can compromise our purpose because we run the risk of living a life that clashes with the message of the Gospel. "Lest, when I preach to others," challenges us to practice what we preach. Consistency (alignment of message and action) is the result of pursuing a real purpose with a disciplined life. The result is a life that redeems the time. (Ephesians 5:16)

WALK IN VICTORY … *Consistency (alignment of message and action) is the result of pursuing real purpose with a disciplined life. Is there anything in your life that betrays a lack of discipline?*

MIND-ALTERING LIVING: REST

"Come to Me, all you who labor and are heavy laden, and I will give you rest. Take My yoke upon you and learn from Me, for I am gentle and lowly in heart, and you will find rest for your souls. For My yoke is easy and My burden is light."

MATTHEW 11:28-30

Whenever we live a purpose-filled life in the finished work of Jesus, there will be times of weariness. Real purpose still produces weariness because real purpose is not easy. The resulting outlook is a tired body with a willing spirit. God's plan for His people is to lead our hearts to a place of rest in Jesus—the One to Whom our hearts belong.

Jesus spoke about this rest to a religious audience in Matthew 11:28, "Come to Me, all you who labor and are heavy laden [burned out by all your religious effort] and I will give you rest." Sometimes we forget the meaning of simple words. This passage has one of those "simple words" that carries immense weight. Think about the word "rest" for a second – what does it mean? Stop working. Take a break. Refresh yourself. Put an end to your efforts. This seems like an odd thing for Jesus to say during a commission to "follow Me." Jesus knows this about religious people—we keep forgetting our effort did not (and will not) make the cut. (Romans 3:23) But because we forget, we tend to put pressure on our efforts to meet the standards of holy living. Then we grow weary. We grow weak in the fight against sin, and we fall victim to pet sins we thought were long gone. We compromise and cut corners to maintain an appearance of purposeful living while drowning in the guilt of living a "double life" because we know that weariness never trumps purpose.

We need a reminder. Jesus has a good one, "It is finished." A mind-altered life rests in Jesus. God rested on the Sabbath day of the week after finishing the work of creation. Jesus rested on the Sabbath day of the week after finishing the work of the cross. So where is our Sabbath rest? His name is Jesus! (Hebrews 4:9-16) Weariness never trumps purpose! Jesus, at the height of His weariness, surrendered willingly to the mission of the cross. Weariness will entice us to "manufacture" rest by abandoning our cross, but this is a false rest. There is no true rest without the cross because there is no power of the resurrection outside of oneness with the suffering of the cross. So how do we institute purposeful rest? By abiding in Christ!

WALK IN VICTORY ... *Have you abandoned the cross (Christ's mission) in a vain attempt to rest? Can true rest exist outside of the mission and life of Christ?*

MIND-ALTERING LIVING: FOCUS

"The lamp of the body is the eye. If therefore your eye is good, your whole body will be full of light. But if your eye is bad, your whole body will be full of darkness ... how great is that darkness!"

MATTHEW 6:22-23

Our gaze determines our focus. Our focus exposes our desires, and our desires betray how we believe we will attain satisfaction. Just as a hunter has a singular desire for the target entering his field of vision, the mind-altered lifestyle gazes on the beauty of Jesus and places His glory in the crosshairs of purpose. But what is the beauty of Jesus, anyway? This phrase can conjure Sunday School images of a blue-sashed Galilean with gentle eyes and flowing locks, but the beauty of Jesus does not refer to His appearance; it is His holiness!

The holiness of God increases our focus because as we zero in on the eternal, the enemy's lies of temporary pleasure grow more and more obvious. The lust of the flesh, the lust of the eyes, and the pride of life begin to lose their grip on your soul when the eyes of your heart behold the uncomplicated beauty of holy living. (1 John 2:15-17) This is why Paul encourages us, "Set your mind on things above, not on things on the earth." (Colossians 3:2)

So how is our focus reset to the right things? Jesus answers. "If therefore your eye is good, your whole body will be full of light. But if your eye is bad, your whole body will be full of darkness..." (Matthew 6:22b-23a) Our eyes easily affect our thinking because our beliefs are often built on the foundation of what we can observe and experience personally. When we continually observe and experience the pleasures of sin (however fleeting), we begin to believe that true satisfaction can only be experienced by gratifying the desires of the flesh. On the other hand, a mind altered by gazing at the holiness of God will discipline us, by grace, to walk by faith and not by sight. (2 Corinthians 5:7) The result is a deeper appreciation for and hotter pursuit of the beauty of Jesus' holiness which deals a crippling blow to the desires of the self-life.

WALK IN VICTORY *... Do not lose focus! Redeem the time!*

"When you kill time, remember that it has no resurrection." — A.W. Tozer

MIND-ALTERING LIVING: PROVISION

"And my God shall supply all your need according to His riches in glory by Christ Jesus."

PHILIPPIANS 4:19

The mind-altered life is secure knowing the source of our provision is Jesus Christ. This is more than a passive "head knowledge"—it is a truth that gives us His peace! This peace confidently battles against the hopeless mindsets of worry, anxiety, fear, lack of confidence, dissatisfaction, prayerlessness, and materialism. Think about it: How could the enemy attack a contented soul? God's provision fortifies our contentment!

"And my God" … This is a personal relationship with a personal God. There is no wondering, *"Who is this God?"* because He has revealed Himself to us in the pages of His Word! Furthermore, He has invited us to come boldly into His presence to obtain mercy, well-timed help, and any good thing we need! (Hebrews 4:14-16, 10:19-22; Ephesians 3:12; Matthew 7:7-11)

"shall supply" … This is a promise of preparation. When we hear the word "supply" (or "supplies"), we often think of preparing for a mission. Whether it is an afternoon hike, a weekend baseball tournament, an early morning hunt, or a desperate situation in a hotly contested warzone, we all want to feel equipped for the assignment. God meets us in our mission and confidently reassures us, *"I have what you need to succeed today."* (Psalm 23:1)

"all your need" … This is a knowledge of necessity. God does not need to guess what we need or speculate about how much we need. We will never look at the gifts of God with sanctified vision and say, "I have all I need of this, thank you" or "I think You gave me the wrong gift." We will never need a gift receipt to return something unnecessary or return to His table for second helpings—His initial provision is *all* we need! (2 Peter 1:3)

"according to His riches in glory by Christ Jesus" … This is the mind-altering means of provision. Up to this point, we could easily rip this verse out of context and start claiming all sorts of "needs," but this final clause provides us with the "checks and balances" for a wandering heart. Jesus is our provision, and God will meet every need in Jesus. Will He also provide financially? Yes! Good health? Yes! Safety and comfort? Of course! But when the finances grow thin, our health fails, and suffering disrupts our lives, has God stopped providing? Not by a long shot! On those days, our abundant spiritual provision is *even more* meaningful! Jesus is with us. Jesus is fighting for us. Jesus is our access to the Father and He has *all* we need!

WALK IN VICTORY … *Think back over the past year—how did God provide for you? Meditate on the goodness of God and thank Him for His provision!*

MIND-ALTERING LIVING: OBEDIENCE

"If you love Me, keep My commandments …
he who does not love Me does not keep My words."

JOHN 14:15, 24

The mind-altered lifestyle finds great joy and pleasure in obedience because, in God's economy, true obedience is the natural overflow of loving God! Most people wince at this because we have become convinced there is meaningful pleasure in hollow, momentary things (disobedience). But to find true joy-filled, God-honoring pleasure in our obedience, we must be willing to die to the fleeting affections of the flesh. Sentencing the self-life to death will grow our love and, by extension, help us grow into *"no matter what"* obedience! Consider the *"no matter what"* obedience of our Lord Jesus Christ in Philippians 2:8, "He humbled Himself and became obedient to the point of death, even the death of the cross." Hebrews 12:2 tells us Jesus executed *"no matter what"* obedience "for the joy that was set before Him." His love for the Father and pursuit of real joy motivated Him to a cross that would open the gate for all of us to experience authentic, joy-filled obedience! But how do we know our obedience is full of joy and flowing from an authentic love for God? How can we avoid the exhausting quicksand of legalistic moralism? Consider the following:

OBEDIENCE SATISFIES … Authentic obedience flows from an authentic love for our Master. Satisfied peace floods our hearts as we simply do what He tells us to do because we know our Master will be pleased with our work. (John 2:5, 2 Timothy 2:3-4)

OBEDIENCE SUSTAINS … Obedience is not authentic if it is only done halfway or half-heartedly. In this sense, authentic, love-based obedience sustains us to persevere until the finish line. Paul, nearing the end of his life, highlights the sustaining power of obedience this way: "I have fought the good fight, I have finished the race, I have kept the faith." (2 Timothy 4:7)

OBEDIENCE STRENGTHENS … The enemy has persuaded far too many saints that obedience is draining drudgery. Problematically, this logic also dictates we might find strength in our disobedience. Remember, Christian, "it is no longer I who live, but Christ lives in me..." (Galatians 2:20) There is no greater strength than the power of the Holy Spirit living within us to obey the Gospel! (Acts 1:8, Romans 1:5)

OBEDIENCE SEES THE NEED ... Jesus once instructed the twelve to "lift up your eyes" and see the fields are "[*ready*] for harvest!" (John 4:35) If obedience is a draining drudgery, we will never want to see the needs around us because it poses a threat to our comfort—hard work.

OBEDIENCE SEIZES THE OPPORTUNITY ... The instruction to "see the need" is essentially an instruction to do something about it. Authentic obedience is *never* satisfied with simply observing an opportunity! (Luke 10:25-37) That does not mean every need is for every person, but each one of us must observe the "field" within our reach. Is the harvest ready?

WALK IN VICTORY ... *Is your life in Christ marked by "no matter what" obedience? Evaluate your life using the five characteristics of authentic obedience.*

PICKING THE RIGHT PATH

"You will show me the path of life; In Your presence is fullness of joy; At Your right hand are pleasures forevermore."

PSALM 16:11

Life can be rough and tumble—especially if you're on the wrong path! Jesus said that each of us has to choose which "path" or "way" we will walk in life. (Matthew 7:13-14) Whether you realize it or not, each one of us is already on a path right now. How can we know we are walking on the right path today? Let's examine Psalm 16:11 to see the great benefits of the right path.

A PERSONAL PATH … Notice the personal pronouns "You" and "me" used throughout this verse. The right path is a personal relationship with the Lord! Jesus said that the right path is narrow and difficult (even impossible) to navigate without Him, and the only way in is by entering the "narrow gate" by faith. (Matthew 7:13-14) There is no mystery here. Jesus calls Himself "the door" (or "gate") in John 10:9 *and* "the way" in John 14:6. In other words, the right path *begins* and *continues* with a personal relationship with Christ!

A PURPOSEFUL PATH … "You will show me the path of life…" The Lord has a purpose (or "will") for your life. God's purposeful path for you will only be known through a personal relationship with the Lord and daily communion in His Word and presence (prayer). Friend, there is no greater purpose for life than to follow and serve the Lord! What else will matter for eternity? *ABSOLUTELY NOTHING!* There is no lasting purpose in life apart from the Lord because He created you to love and represent Him.

A PRIVILEGED PATH … "In Your presence is fullness of joy…" The right path is a place where we can be in the presence of Almighty God! Is there a greater privilege? Do you experience the awesome fulfillment and joy of being in the presence of the Lord daily? We commune with the God of the universe through His indwelling Holy Spirit! What a privilege!

A PLEASURABLE PATH … "At Your right hand are pleasures forevermore." You cannot know real pleasure until you walk on the right path with the Lord! This is not a life free of difficulty, but a life where we have peace, joy, and communion with God. It gets better! We also know that one day, we will dwell *forever* in perfect, sinless pleasure. The pleasure of the right path is abundant *and* eternal! (Revelation 21:1-5) Praise God!

WALK IN VICTORY *… Consider this statement: "You cannot know real pleasure until you walk on the right path with the Lord." Do you agree or disagree? Why?*

PURITY: PURSUING A POSITION IN PRACTICE

"And everyone who has this hope in Him purifies himself, just as He is pure."

1 JOHN 3:3

Some of the most widely misunderstood concepts in the Old Testament are the purity laws. Normal things in our modern lives are labeled "unclean" or "impure" to an ancient Israelite. These laws often cause modern readers to respond negatively, but to be "pure" or "clean" was protection, not punishment! To be near God's completely pure, holy presence, you needed to be "clean." God established the process for ritual purification to restore nearness—a real relationship! In the New Testament, the mark of a Christian is a life of inside-out purity. The Holy Spirit, indwelling all believers, ensures a position of purity before God, but the Christian must also *pursue* purity in *practice*. The question then becomes, *"How do we live a life of purity in an evil day?"*

Physical Purity ... God expects us to live a physically pure life! In 1 Thessalonians 4:3-8, the Apostle Paul assures us we will endure constant temptation. The corrupted message and empty promises of sexual immorality bombard us all the time. The world is constantly relaying the message that pursuing sexual fulfillment outside of marriage is not only normal but celebrated. As 1 Thessalonians states, "For this is the will of God, your sanctification: that you should abstain from sexual immorality." (4:3) God's will is the practice of holiness, and in our bodies, that means physical purity.

Mental Purity ... Not only does God expect us to live a physically pure life, but He expects mental purity. Philippians 4:7-8 teaches if we are going to be pure vessels, we must keep our minds out of the gutter. What we put into our minds affects who we are and how we live! We *cannot* fill our minds with the opinions of the world and expect to have clean minds. We must continually cleanse our minds with the truths of the Word of God. (See James 4:8; Romans 12:1-2) Is your mind pure before the Lord?

Spiritual Purity ... Lastly, we must keep ourselves spiritually pure; that is, we should not be consumed by the desires of the flesh or the lies of the enemy. Christian, just as you are *already* victorious in Christ, you are *also already* pure! (Romans 5:1, 8:1) As we yield ourselves completely to God, our position of purity in Christ becomes the reality of our practice! To practice *impurity* is to deny who you are in Christ! (James 4:4) A life pursuing spiritual purity loves the Lord by keeping His commands! (1 John 5:1-5)

WALK IN VICTORY ... *Are you actively pursuing purity in these three areas of Christian practice? (1 Thessalonians 4:3-8)*

SEVEN ELEMENTS OF RIGHTEOUSNESS

"But now the righteousness of God apart from the law is revealed … even the righteousness of God, through faith in Jesus Christ, to all and on all who believe."

ROMANS 3:21-22

What is righteousness? Simply put, it is "right standing" before God. This righteousness is an unearned, gracious gift of God through salvation in the Lord Jesus Christ. In fact, the righteousness we have as followers of Jesus is more than a gift *from* Jesus—it's *HIS* right standing practically applied to us through His indwelling Holy Spirit! (More on that later!) The Apostle Paul spent a lot of time and effort writing about the gift of Christ's righteousness and the effects of His righteousness on the life of a surrendered Christian. Today, we will examine seven elements of righteousness from the Apostle Paul's letter to the believers in Rome.

[Read Romans 3:20-31]

Our Righteousness is Apart from the Law … The law of God was given to know sin and understand what goes against God's character. (v.20) God never intended to use the law as a measuring stick by which sinners would eventually become savable. The law condemns! You cannot earn your way into right standing before God.

Our Righteousness is Revealed in the Scripture … "The Law and the Prophets" was a way of summarizing the teaching of the Jewish faith (what we call the "Old Testament"). Paul tells us that God's righteousness is not a new thing. He has always been righteous and has always demanded right living.

Our Righteousness is Imputed by Faith … The righteousness of Christ is credited to the account of all who believe in Jesus as Lord and Savior! His right standing with God is applied to you by faith, not works.

Our Righteousness is Provided for All … God did not just provide a path of righteousness to one people group. "There is no difference" between the Jew and the Gentile, Paul says. (v.22) "All have sinned" (v.23), so all have the opportunity to call on the name of the Lord Jesus and be saved!

Our Righteousness is Given Freely by Grace … "Being justified [made righteous] freely by His grace…" (v.24) We are made righteous without a cost. You cannot buy right standing with God. You cannot "climb the mountain" to get to God. He has come down to us—that's *AMAZING* grace!

Our Righteousness is Accomplished through Redemption ... Though we have received this gift freely because of grace, someone had to purchase that gift before it was given. "You were bought with a price," Paul says in 1 Corinthians 6:20. The gift is free to the recipient, but costly for the giver. "Redemption" means we have been "bought back" from the slave block of sin and death and given freedom and life!

Our Righteousness is Paid through Propitiation ... The cost of our redemption was the atoning sacrifice of the Lord Jesus Christ. "For He made Him who knew no sin to be sin for us, that we might become the righteousness of God in Him." (2 Corinthians 5:21)

WALK IN VICTORY ... *If you have been made right with God through Jesus, you cannot be "unmade" through your sinful mistakes. You are free! Live in victory today!*

Sing the song "Amazing Grace" to close out your time in the Word today.

REAL ZEAL

"Now when Phinehas the son of Eleazar, the son of Aaron the priest, saw it, he rose from among the congregation and took a javelin in his hand…"

NUMBERS 25:7

Zeal (that is, intense passion) is not a *missing* character trait in modern life, but it is often *misguided*. Unfortunately, most of the zeal we see today is unchecked selfishness or undisciplined cowardice. Some are zealous about never picking a side. I call them the "Fence Sitters." They believe there is safety by never revealing what they think about anything. They would call this being "diplomatic" or even "loving." But true diplomacy recognizes an enemy of good and always stands for what is true. Some are zealous about *never* being zealous. They see passionate people as reckless and hasty. I call this type "The Hiders." Every time there is a conflict of any kind, they disappear. *"Don't get involved!"* That's their motto. But what about *real* zeal? Doesn't God want us to be passionate about His glory? *ABSOLUTELY!*

One of the best examples of a man zealous for God is found in Numbers 25. In this passage, the women of Moab lured the Israelites into the idolatrous, sexualized worship of the false god, Baal. God was extremely angry with this unashamed betrayal by "His people." He was their God, and they were to "image" Him to their unbelieving neighbors. They had broken the covenant, so He told Moses to execute every chief of Israel who had participated in the idolatry. On top of that, God disciplined the Israelite people with a deadly plague that slew 24,000. As these sentences were being carried out, some Israelites began weeping in repentance at the Tabernacle, but Salu (an Israelite leader) foolishly continued in sin as he escorted a Midianite woman through the mourners and into his tent. Seeing this, Phinehas, the son of Eleazar the High Priest, was enraged by Salu's blatant disrespect for God! He grabbed a spear, burst into the tent, and pinned both the man and the woman to the ground by piercing them through the gut!

What would possess Phinehas to do something so bold? Wasn't his zealous response too hasty? Was he being unfair or unjust? Not according to God! "Then the Lord spoke to Moses, saying: 'Phinehas the son of Eleazar, the son of Aaron the priest, has turned back My wrath from the children of Israel, because he was zealous with My zeal among them...'" (25:10-11) Wow! What an incredible commendation from the Lord! But how did this action show real zeal?

Real zeal is trained by God. Phinehas was "the son of Eleazar, the son of Aaron the priest." (v.7) His family's legacy of faith (and sometimes misplaced zeal – *see Leviticus 10*) along with his priestly training was a major factor in his willingness to be zealous for the Lord! Real zeal also has trained sight. Phinehas recognized the sin before him and saw it for what it was—open rebellion against God! The ability to clearly define sin is too often missing in our lives, and it keeps us from being zealous for the Lord. Real zeal doesn't sit on the fence—it takes a stand and acts! "He rose from among the congregation and took a javelin in his hand…" (v.7) Phinehas radically dealt with sin and made sure public consequences were known. Real zeal is motivated by God's glory and acts in God's strength—this is the only way real zeal produces God's blessing! (v.11-13) Do you desire the blessing of living for the Lord with *real* zeal? Live for the glory of God above all else!

WALK IN VICTORY … *How did the Lord Jesus model Real Zeal for God's glory in radically dealing with your sin?*

Review the full story of "Real Zeal" by reading Numbers 25.

Review the story of "misplaced zeal" by some of Phinehas' relatives in Leviticus 10:1-11.

RUNNING THE RACE

"Therefore we also, since we are surrounded by so great a cloud of witnesses, let us lay aside every weight, and the sin which so easily ensnares us, and let us run with endurance the race that is set before us, looking unto Jesus, the author and finisher of our faith, who for the joy that was set before Him endured the cross, despising the shame, and has sat down at the right hand of the throne of God."

HEBREWS 12:1-2

We must be actively engaged in "running the race" of the Christian life because we have an enemy who is actively opposing our running! We are constantly tempted to stop running or run in the wrong direction. Both of these would bring us back into bondage!

What does it mean to stop running? We stop running when we become overloaded by dead weight. (v.1) If we are going to run effectively, we must lose all weighty distractions. I see two sources of dead weight in this passage: (1) The Weight Which Slows and (2) The Weight Which Sins. The weights which slow us down are not fundamentally sinful, but anything that diverts our attention, saps our energy, and dampens our enthusiasm can easily become sinful! *"What's wrong with that?"* is the wrong question to ask of these weights. Instead, we must ask, *"Does it help me run?"* On the other hand, the weightiness of sin is bondage. We cannot run if we are tied up and in bondage to sin! Does anything hinder your running today? What is slowing you down or keeping you bound?

Effective runners must look ahead to the pace-setters who have run ahead! (v.1) These "witnesses" are not passive watchers, they are examples! Run as they did! These witnesses ran faithfully. They never stopped running as they trusted the Savior. They ran fervently—running through the finish line with *all* their might! Our forerunners also ran fiercely with overwhelming courage.

Finally, my fellow runners, we must keep our eyes on The Winner—our Lord and Savior Jesus Christ! (v.2) To have our course laid before us by The Winner of the Great Race of Faith is both challenging and intimidating! His pace and path are the proper focus! But be watchful! We do not run without distractions. Our focus can often be tempted away toward self ("What pleases me?"), others ("What pleases them?"), and the world ("Why please God?"). Fight back against these distractions! "For consider Him Who endured such hostility from sinners against Himself, lest you become weary and discouraged in your souls." (Hebrews 12:3)

WALK IN VICTORY ... *Further "running" study in scripture: Genesis 39:1-12; 1 Corinthians 9:24-27; Galatians 5:7; Philippians 2:14-16*

SEIZING NEW HEIGHTS

"Now therefore, give me this mountain of which the Lord spoke in that day… It may be that the Lord will be with me, and I shall be able to drive them out as the Lord said."

JOSHUA 14:10-12

As the Promised Land was being assigned to each Israelite tribe, Caleb steps forward to make a bold request of his faithful friend, Joshua. Caleb wanted a particular land—the land of Hebron. This request was not only bold, but it was incredibly risky! This land had not been secured—the enemy was everywhere and still held firm control. Caleb was also 85 years old! Now don't give me any of that "85 in Bible years" stuff because Moses lived to 120 and Joshua dies at 110! Caleb's 85 is still old, but it doesn't matter to him. This 85-year-old warrior is trusting God to empower him to stay in the battle!

God is pleased to help us pursue bold faith! There are more than a few examples in the Bible. Moses declares, "Show me Your glory!" (Exodus 33) David boldly threatens Goliath in 1 Samuel 17. The Gentile centurion and water-walking Peter exercise bold faith! (Matthew 8:8, 14:28-29) The Lord honors bold faith! But to exercise bold faith and seize new heights, one must ascend the mountains of preparation along the way. Notice some of the mountains of preparation that Caleb ascended in his life:

[Read Numbers 13:1-14:24]

When God instructed Moses to scout the Promised Land, Joshua and Caleb were the only men who obediently accomplished the task and gave a trustworthy report. As a result, Joshua and Caleb were trusted by the Lord! One who is faithful in small tasks will indeed be trusted with great responsibilities! (Matthew 25:21; Luke 16:10) Caleb had great faith in the Lord! He trusted God's promises because he knew God's character. Bold faith will be born out of saturating ourselves in the Word of God. It amazes me how many Christians today fill their minds with everything *except* God's Word! No wonder we are so easily swayed into weak faith! This is where, like Caleb, we must ascend the preparing mountain of opposition. Whenever you do anything for the Lord and act in bold faith, expect the naysayers! There will *always* be opposition to obeying the Lord. To live in bold faith, you must be willing to face stiff opposition, discouragement, and struggle! How will you respond? (See Numbers 13:30, 14:24)

WALK IN VICTORY … *What are you trusting God to do in your life through bold faith? Are you allowing God to prepare you through these "character-building" mountains? Your family will greatly benefit from your bold obedience! (Joshua 14:13-15)*

VICTORY!

THANKS BE TO GOD!

"But thanks be to God, who gives us the victory through our Lord Jesus Christ."

1 CORINTHIANS 15:57

"In Congress, July 4, 1776"

This is the bold heading at the top of the most well-known print of America's Declaration of Independence. The supersized signature of John Hancock joins 55 other founding fathers as the decisive seal at the bottom of the page. This historic document, including its 27 grievances against King George III, stands as a symbol for the American people. In a sense, the Declaration of Independence stated, "We know who we are, and we know how we are supposed to live!" While imperfect in its execution, the sentiments are beautiful, good, and true. Similarly, the Word of God has given us several declarations of victory over the tyranny of our former life as slaves of sin. Though our execution is imperfect, these truths are beautiful, good, and true. Today, we are going to affirm the declarations of the victorious Christian life:

I have abundant life! (John 10:10)

I cannot out-sin the grace of God! (Romans 5:20)

I am no longer condemned because of Christ Jesus! (Romans 8:1)

I am justified! (Romans 8:30)

I am unfinished, but I will one day be perfected! (Romans 8:30)

I am confident in the face of any foe because God is for me! (Romans 8:31)

I am more than a conqueror in Christ Jesus! (Romans 8:37)

I cannot be separated from God's love! (Romans 8:38-39)

I am accepted because I am in Christ! (Ephesians 1:6)

I am sealed by the Holy Spirit until the day of redemption! (Ephesians 1:13, 4:30)

I do not have to be afraid! (1 John 4:18)

I am loved by God! (1 John 4:19)

I am an overcomer in Christ! The world is powerless against me! (1 John 5:4-5)

I know where I will spend eternity! (Revelation 21:1-4)

WALK IN VICTORY ... *"Though our execution is imperfect, these truths are beautiful, good, and true." The truth is true whether or not you believe it! Christian, live victoriously! Live the TRUTH! (Bookmark this page and revisit it often!)*

THANKFULNESS

"Rejoice always, pray without ceasing, in everything give thanks; for this is the will of God in Christ Jesus for you."

1 THESSALONIANS 5:16-18

Thankfulness is an Expression of Praise ... (Psalm 100) When we have acknowledged the greatness of our Lord and seen ourselves for who we are, it motivates us to praise the Lord with a heart filled with thanks! When we thank the Lord, it turns our hearts to worship!

Thankfulness is an Expression of Posture ... (Luke 17:11-15) Notice the posture of this Samaritan—here is thankfulness in prayer! A thankful person reveals the humble posture of his heart, but an ungrateful person is revealing the fruit of a proud heart. When we express thanks, we are acknowledging our utter dependence on God. A grateful heart expresses humility; it bows low before a mighty God!

Thankfulness is an Element of Purpose ... (1 Thessalonians 5:18) "In everything give thanks; *for this is the will of God* in Christ Jesus for you." (emphasis added) Do you want to know God's will? Here is one aspect of His will—GIVE THANKS! Giving thanks in prayer molds our perspective to view life the way God does. It helps us think with the mind of Christ! It might not be easy to give thanks "in everything," but when we do, we practice the renewal of the mind to think and live in the will of God. (Romans 12:1-2)

Thankfulness is an Element of Peace ... (Philippians 4:6-7) A grateful heart produces peace and comfort in a world of turmoil and confusion. When we practice gratitude towards God, His peace overwhelms the soul even in the most difficult circumstances! If you need peace amid conflict or difficulty, practice giving thanks to God!

Thankfulness is an Element of Protection ... (Philippians 4:6-8) A grateful heart shields us from the enemy who always attacks our thinking and feeling. An ungrateful mindset and heart attitude results in murmuring and complaining which compromises the light of the Gospel. (Philippians 2:14-15)

Thankfulness is an Expression that MUST be Practiced ... (Luke 17:11-15) Only one out of ten practiced thankfulness. Sadly, most Christians practice thanklessness far more than thankfulness. If we desire to be humble servants of the Lord, we *must practice* thankfulness! We have been given much. A selfish attitude of *"I deserve this"* is an easy trap. We need to establish thankfulness as a daily habit.

WALK IN VICTORY ... *Are you living in God's will with a thankful heart today?*

THE CHRISTIAN'S MISSION

"But you shall receive power when the Holy Spirit has come upon you; and you shall be witnesses to Me in Jerusalem, and in all Judea and Samaria, and to the end of the earth."

ACTS 1:8

Every Christian has been called, commanded, and commissioned to reach the lost with the message of Jesus Christ! This is the mission of *every* Christian! Often, when someone obeys this command on a global level, we refer to it as "missions." By taking the word "mission" (that applies to *every* Christian) and selectively using it for people who obey the mission globally, we tend to let ourselves off the hook! But the Christian mission is not just for "missionaries!" It is for *ALL* Christians in *ALL* locations at *ALL* times!

The Power of Missions – "But you shall receive power..." The power to accomplish the Christian mission is not our own, but the power of the Holy Spirit working in us! Human determination alone cannot accomplish this monumental task! Our flesh is weak and loves comfort, but our mission is anything but comfortable! It demands total surrender to the power of God! A surrendered life cannot help but share the Gospel! (Acts 4:20)

The Privilege of Missions – "and you shall be witnesses to Me..." Every Christian has the responsibility and privilege to share the Word of God! If we neglect this responsibility, how will people come to Christ? (Romans 10:14-15) It is a privilege to take the witness stand for the Lord!

The Personal Blessing of Missions – "in Jerusalem, and in all Judea and Samaria, and to the end of the earth." One of the great truths of the Bible is that there is overwhelming joy in Heaven every time someone turns to the Savior for salvation! (Luke 15:7) The personal blessing of missions comes from personally owning this responsibility in our "Jerusalem"—that is, the people in our hometown! See? Even Acts 1:8 sees "missions" as a local responsibility *as well as* a global responsibility. There is great blessing in owning the mission!

The Priesthood of Missions – (1 Peter 2:9) "But you are a chosen generation, a royal priesthood, a holy nation, His own special people, that you may proclaim the praises of Him who called you out of darkness into His marvelous light." The basic work of a priest is to proclaim the Person and Word of God. Their goal was to bring great honor to the Lord because He is worthy of our praise! The priestly work of every believer is to bear the message of His marvelous light to a world lost in utter darkness.

WALK IN VICTORY ... *Have you personally owned the responsibility of the Christian mission on a local level? Have you asked the Lord if He desires to expand the territory of His mission in your life?*

THE GREAT EXCHANGE

"God made Him who had no sin to be sin for us, so that in Him we might become the righteousness of God."

2 CORINTHIANS 5:21

If you could exchange anything in your life for something else, what would that exchange look like? A boring job for an exciting job? Crippling debt for a full bank account? Bad grades for straight A's? How about exchanging a gut for rippling muscles! Our initial reactions often lack imagination or meaningful life change. Ironically, the greatest exchange ever made has little effect on the things mentioned above! God made sinless Jesus to become our sin so that in Jesus we could become the righteousness of God. What a glorious exchange! Have you considered the magnitude of this exchange?

Exchange Sin for Righteousness ... Every person is a sinner who falls short of God's holy character—the standard of right and wrong. (Romans 3:23) You might say, "Hey, I'm a pretty good person!" You might even be a better person than me! But I'm not the standard—God is! James 1:10 tells us that even breaking just ONE of God's laws makes you a sinner! "Well, that's not fair!" Is it unfair? Is it fair that one broken law is enough to put someone in prison? (What if that broken law affected you?) It seems that fairness isn't the question here. We just don't like knowing the truth about our sin! But here's the good news: when we accept Jesus Christ and His finished work on the cross, we can exchange our sin for His righteousness!

Exchange Death for Life ... We are sinners, and the penalty for our sin is death. (Romans 6:23) This death is eternal separation from God in hell. When we accept Jesus as our Lord and Savior, we exchange death (the rightly-owed payment for sin paid through the death of the Lord Jesus) for life! This new life in Christ is eternal and abundant! (John 10:10)

Exchange Emptiness for Fulfillment ... Receiving Jesus Christ as Lord and Savior will give you purpose and fulfillment! That abundant life mentioned in John 10:10 is the only life worth living because it lives on past this temporary life! Even if you had an exciting job, a full bank account, supreme intellect, and rippling muscles, ALL of that will be gone the moment you enter eternity.

Exchange Slavery for Sonship ... When you receive Jesus as Lord and Savior, God exchanges your bankrupt slavery for abundant sonship! Galatians 4:6-7 says it this way, "And because you are sons, God has sent forth the Spirit of His Son into your hearts, crying out, 'Abba, Father!' Therefore, you are no longer a slave but a son, and if a son, then an heir of God through Christ."

WALK IN VICTORY ... *What does this exchange mean for your life today?*

THE HIGHWAY OF HOLINESS

"Be holy, for I am holy."

1 PETER 1:15-16

When God forgives our sins and unites us with Christ, several incredible transformations take place in our lives. One of God's greatest gifts of grace is the status of being "holy" or "pure" before the Lord! (Colossians 3:12) This is not just a passive status, but a new identity! Sadly, even with this new identity, the practical changes in our behavior can be slow and inconsistent. When you read the verse above from Peter commanding us to "Be holy," he might as well be saying "Be able to fly!" How do we measure up to this expectation of holiness? How do we obey our Lord's command?

The first thing to remember about the highway of holiness is that we are living in a new reality. I use the word "highway" on purpose as a connection to an illustration. When you drive on a highway you will often see signage that tells you where you will end up if you continue driving on that road. The sign isn't trying to tell you that you have arrived—only that you are heading in the right direction if the place listed on the sign is your destination. "This is the right road! Just keep driving!" I know of one road on the way home where the sign reads "Roanoke" almost 100 miles before I arrive! I've never once stopped by that sign and thought, *"Well, here it is! I'm home now!"* Are you starting to get the picture of how this helps us think about holiness? (1) I am on the right road, heading in the right direction. (2) I am always getting closer to home! (3) With patient endurance, I will one day arrive home!

Now think spiritually with me! (1) *Positional Holiness*: We have been freed from the penalty of sin! We are on the right road and are now headed in the right direction! We *are on* the path of holiness right now, which means we *are* holy! There is no other way to *walk* in holiness than to *be* holy. But we're not home yet! (2) *Practical Holiness*: We have been freed from the power of sin! As we continue on the highway of holiness, we draw closer to home. Sin is now powerless to control us and cannot force us to turn away from our holy destination. Even a temporary lapse in sin does not derail the long-term path. Our holy destination is certain to those who are in Christ Jesus because you cannot out-sin grace! Keep driving in "victory lane!" (3) *Perfected Holiness*: One day, we will be HOME! We will be freed from the presence of sin and our holiness will be complete in the new creation with our resurrected bodies!

With this in mind, which statement is most correct? I am Holy. (Hebrews 10:10, 14) I am striving to live a holy life. (Matthew 5:48) One day, I will be holy. (1 Thessalonians 5:23-24) … *ALL* are Biblically correct!

WALK IN VICTORY … *By God's grace, are you practicing holiness in Christ Jesus?*

REPENTANCE: JOY FROM GODLY SORROW

"Godly sorrow brings repentance that leads to salvation..."

2 CORINTHIANS 7:10

The Holy Spirit moves us to recognize sin for what it is and reject its deceptive promises. This is a change of mind, or "turning" from sin. (Also called "repentance.") Matthew 3:2 and 3:8 summarize the "why" for repentance this way: "Repent, for the kingdom of heaven is at hand! ...Therefore, bear fruits worthy of repentance." Repentance bears the joyful fruit of "turning" from the seeds of godly sorrow over sin. In 2 Corinthians 7:8-12, at least 8 joy-filled "fruits" of genuine repentance are mentioned:

"DILIGENCE" ... One of the first fruits of a repented believer is a diligence or eager desire to seek righteousness. The individual becomes convicted by the Holy Spirit to deal with sin quickly and completely. When he realizes sin is breaking fellowship with the Lord, he addresses it immediately.

"CLEARING OF YOURSELF" ... Repentance is eager to clear the conscience. Repentance keeps a short sin account because a changed mind eagerly desires to disassociate itself from sin.

"INDIGNATION" ... Repentance leads to righteous or holy anger towards sin and its shame. This anger is manifested in sincere displeasure for sin and the way it affects fellowship with the Lord and others.

"FEAR" ... In other words, "alarm!" Repentance realizes that God is chiefly offended by sin. A changed mind is alarmed that His Holy Lord has been offended. He eagerly seeks reconciliation with the Lord.

"VEHEMENT DESIRE" ... A change of mind increases our desire to maintain right fellowship with the Lord and others. The "strong desire" is for ongoing reconciliation within these relationships.

"ZEAL" ... Repentance zealously loves the Lord and fellow believers. The zealous believer does not excuse sin and acknowledges its destructive ways. He is passionate about dealing with sin quickly.

"VINDICATION" ... A changed mind no longer tries to protect, cover, or justify his sin. Sin needs to be dealt with completely, no matter the cost! This is true humility in action.

"CLEAR IN THIS MATTER" ... Repentance brings an aggressive pursuit of holiness. Purity through the pursuit of holiness maintains a clear conscience between the repentant believer, God, and fellow believers.

WALK IN VICTORY ... *Are the joy-filled fruits of repentance alive in your life?*

73

THE MINDSET OF DEATH

"Let this mind be in you which was also in Christ Jesus."

PHILIPPIANS 2:5

When the Lord Jesus Christ walked on this earth, He did so with a mindset of death. What? Jesus had a mindset of death? I thought He was here to give abundant life! (John 10:10) That's exactly right! But to give us life, Christ had to give up His life. This is the true essence of humility—death to self. Christ was committed to dying because He knew His death would glorify The Father. (John 10:17-18) He humbled Himself and modeled the mindset of "dying to self" by living out the perfect will of God the Father. (Luke 22:42) That kind of commitment is unwavering because it is *FILLED* with purpose!

[Read Philippians 2:1-11]

The humility of the Lord Jesus can be seen in His unwavering sacrifice. Jesus emptied Himself of the advantages and privileges of His heavenly home to live among us. (Philippians 2:5-7) What an incredible sacrifice! Are we willing to obey our Heavenly Father, no matter the cost?

This mindset also produces unwavering service. Jesus took on flesh to identify with our hardship and model a life of unwavering human service to God. As a man, Christ did not live in luxury and comfort. He took on the position of a bondservant—the lowest position available—and was obedient to the point of death. He not only served His Father through dying but also served sinners through His death and resurrection! (Romans 5:8) This is not a natural mindset; it is supernatural!

What about us? God has called and equipped every Christian to take up his cross, die to self, and follow Christ's example. (Luke 9:23) This call builds in us an unwavering responsibility to the Lord Jesus Christ! How can we say "no" to a Lord Who modeled "death to self" first? We have a responsibility as good soldiers of the cross to carry our cross in selfless humility and love, just as Christ did. (Philippians 2:8)

WALK IN VICTORY *… Is the mind of Christ evident through your sacrificial service to God and others? Meditate on the unwavering mindset of Jesus in Philippians 2:1-11.*

THE POWER OF WORDS

"And the tongue is a fire, a world of iniquity … and it is set on fire by hell."

JAMES 3:6

James 3 has quite a bit to say to both the "talkers" and the quiet types about the power of words. Technology has greatly expanded the power of the spoken and written word through social media, texting, video chats, and more. Whether it's yelling and screaming or venomous words through a polite tone and polished smile, the tongue is a killer! *"Sticks and stones may break my bones, but words can never hurt me."* This is a nice motto, but it's simply untrue! Words can build or destroy, so how do we use our words well?

THE POWER OF THE TONGUE … James 3:1-8 – Why do you think James starts a discussion about the tongue by talking about teaching? The teacher can use his tongue to build up, tear down, instruct, direct, or lead astray. If you want to examine your spiritual maturity, examine your communication! (v.2) The tongue is given some striking visual comparisons in this passage—including a fire (v.6) untamable beast (v.7), unruly evil (v.8), and a deadly poison! (v.8) Clearly, if you can handle your words, you are a mature believer!

THE PERSONALITY OF THE TONGUE … James 3:9-12 – The same tongue blesses and curses, sometimes in the same sentence! One minute you are praising God, and the next minute you are gossiping about a fellow Christian. One minute you are building up, then tearing down the next! "Man, I liked the music today! … Boy, that sermon was horrible!" This is wildly inconsistent with God's undivided character.

THE PROBLEM OF THE TONGUE … James 3:13-16 – Why is the tongue such a problem? When the tongue is out of order, it proves you are yielding to the flesh! Destructive speech is the fruit of a life that is self-governed instead of Spirit-led. Words designed to hurt, tear down, and "prove your point" are the result of pride. My friend, this is not spiritual; it is evil. (v.16)

THE POWER TO CHANGE … James 3:17-18 – There is hope! We do not have to live or communicate in defeat! Life-giving words are God's design for building up and encouraging His body—especially through singing! (Colossians 3:12-17) These verses describe a Spirit-controlled life (and tongue) as compassionate, kind, humble, gentle, patient, forgiving, loving, unifying, peaceful, thankful, encouraging, evangelistic, musical, grateful, and dedicated to the Lord Jesus.

WALK IN VICTORY … *Do you use your words well? Would others agree?*

THE STEPS OF A GOOD MAN

"The steps of a good man are ordered by the Lord, and He delights in his way.
Though he fall, he shall not be utterly cast down;
For the Lord upholds him with His hand."

PSALM 37:23-24

When you look at images from the terrorist attack of September 11, 2001, the wickedness, death, and destruction is hard to process. Evil is, at times, incomprehensible. Why do those who practice such wickedness seem to prosper? In Psalm 37, David contrasts the good or "righteous" man with the evil or "wicked" man. He asks hard questions and marks the guiding principles of "good" men—especially how good men can (and *should*) respond to wickedness in an evil day.

DO NOT LIVE IN ANGER ... (vv.1-2, 5-8) To live in a spirit of "fret" or anger about the actions of the wicked gives them control over your life! You are placing yourself in bondage to their behavior. Getting worked up about these evil-doers is hard on the good man. "It only causes harm." (v.8)

DO NOT ENVY THEM ... (vv.9-15, 28, 35-38) While the wicked often experience short-term success, it will soon be cut off! If your value system has changed as a result of your new life in the Lord Jesus, why would you need *their* version of success? They have no inheritance! They are being manipulated by the enemy, and are lost without Christ. They need deliverance, not celebration. (Romans 6:13; Ephesians 6:12)

TRUST IN THE LORD AND DO GOOD ... (vv.3, 27, 30-31) Trust means you are willing to delegate the weightiness of life to another. In this way, "fret" is contrasted with faith which is manifested in good works (love). The wicked trust in themselves, and do bad. The child of God trusts in the Lord and does good. What a sharp contrast! The great privilege of faith is the opportunity to dwell (that is, "abide" or "live") in God's presence and enjoy His provision!

DELIGHT IN THE LORD ... (v.4) The Lord the object of our affection and activity! The wicked delight in manmade position and power, but as a child of God, we delight in serving and loving! The unstable power and position of evil-doers are temporary and unsatisfying. (Matthew 20:25-28)

VICTORY!

COMMIT YOUR WAY TO THE LORD … (vv.5-6, 23-24, 39-40) When we walk with God, He directs our path and provides for our lives. We will experience His peace when we understand the satisfaction of His control. God is in control! Trust His plan and commit to following His path!

REST IN THE LORD … (v.7) When we rest in the Lord, God's mind-blowing peace secures our thinking and feeling. (Philippians 4:7) There is great satisfaction and true rest in living life "God's way" instead of trying to figure it out for ourselves. (Proverbs 13:13-16; Matthew 11:28-30)

WALK IN VICTORY … *Are you in bondage because of a spirit of anger? (vv.5-8) If not done already, read through Psalm 37 and take notes below about the paths of the good and the wicked.*

THE WAY OF THE CROSS

"That I may know Him and the power of His resurrection, and the fellowship of His sufferings, being conformed to His death."

PHILIPPIANS 3:10

When I was about 11 years old, I received Christ as my Lord and Savior, but I did not yet know the victory and power available to me! Thankfully, at a very low point in my life, some great men of God began to teach me about the victory I had in Christ! I began to experience "the power of His resurrection." Now that I have grown spiritually, I want more of this resurrection power in my life and ministry! I think American Christianity often limits God to what is "natural" or "possible." My friends, God is *NOT* limited in this way! God is the God of the *IMPOSSIBLE!* Whenever we refuse to exercise God's power in our lives, we miss out! But there is a better way—the way of the cross.

The Way of the Cross is a Personal Relationship … "that I may know Him"
The way of the cross is first and foremost a call to salvation. In America, some have watered down this invitation because they are afraid to offend. But as we will see, the way of the cross is a call to extreme trust and commitment, not some half-hearted prayer. To *really* know God is to first experience His radical salvation!

The Way of the Cross is a Power Revealed … "and the power of His resurrection"
Resurrection power only comes by the way of the cross. To come alive through Christ's life, we must first accept the call to Christ's death. The old man must die! We must be set free from sin to be made alive and free in Him!

The Way of the Cross is a Painful Road … "and the fellowship of His sufferings"
Every true believer has a genuine desire to devote his life to Christ in every way. Romans 12:1-2 says that we have become a "living sacrifice" who crawls up on the altar every day as if to say, "Here I am, Lord! You have ALL of me today!" The way of the cross is painful because it is counter-cultural and unpopular. (Matthew 10:22)

The Way of the Cross is a Perilous Reality … "being conformed to His death"
This is the aspect of identifying with the cross. In Christ's day, the cross was understood as certain death. A genuine believer has identified himself with the cross of Christ! Believer, you have been bought with a price and now you must die to self, just as Christ did, to the glory of God the Father. (1 Corinthians 6:19-20)

WALK IN VICTORY … *Meditate on 1 Corinthians 6:19-20.*

TRAINING WHEELS OR NOT?

"In this you greatly rejoice ... you have been grieved by various trials, that the genuineness of your faith, being much more precious than gold that perishes, though it is tested by fire, may be found to praise, honor, and glory at the revelation of Jesus Christ."

1 PETER 1:6-7

Asa was filled with great expectation and excitement! His fifth birthday was coming up, and his parents had promised to buy him a bicycle. Running late, as usual, his parents were at the store looking at the large selection of shiny bikes. After looking and debating, they finally settled on the bike they knew Asa would like. Asa's mom insisted that they include the training wheels in their purchase, but Asa's dad insisted he didn't need them. After some discussion, mom finally asked, "Why don't you think Asa needs these? Without them, he will never learn to ride this bike." Dad calmly answered, "Because I will teach him to ride by running beside him. This way, Asa will learn that I will be right beside him to catch him when he thinks he is going to fall."

Does it ever feel like God is willing to let you fall under the circumstances and trials of life? As difficult as life might seem, our Lord is always there for us! He has promised to "never leave you nor forsake you." (Hebrews 13:5) The Lord's presence is His greatest and most repeated promise! Especially when life is hard. (Psalm 23:4)

Why do we experience trials? It doesn't seem like the Christian life comes with any training wheels either! God's Word tells us that trials are opportunities for our faith to grow, which ultimately brings Him glory. When we, as His children, live by faith in difficult times, our Father is glorified!

Think about a time in your life when you felt like you were all alone amid a difficult time. With the benefit of hindsight, can you see how your heavenly Father was running alongside you as you "pedaled" forward, by faith, without any training wheels? If you can look back and see God's faithful presence through past trials, you can be confident that you are living by faith in His presence today!

WALK IN VICTORY ... *Will you trust the Lord to grow and purify your faith through hardship? Meditate on the faithfulness of God in Psalm 136 today.*

TRUE FRIENDSHIP

"A man who has friends must himself be friendly;
But there is a friend who sticks closer than a brother."

PROVERBS 18:24

Christian apologist C.S. Lewis once said, "Friendship is unnecessary [because] it has no survival value; rather it is one of those things which give value to survival." The Bible says that to have friends we need to be friendly. Sounds easy enough, right? Not always! In his first season with the Brooklyn Dodgers, Jackie Robinson, the first black man to play Major League baseball, faced unimaginable hate nearly everywhere he traveled. Fastballs were hurled at his head, cleats spiked him on the base paths, and brutal nicknames and insults came flying from opposing dugouts and fans. During one game in Boston, the heckling and racial slurs seemed to reach a fever pitch. In the uproar, another Dodger—a Southern white player named Pee Wee Reese— called a timeout. He walked from his position at shortstop toward Robinson at second base, put his arm around Robinson's shoulder, and stood there with him for what seemed like a long time. One reporter summarized the event this way, "The gesture spoke more eloquently than the words: this man is my friend."

Friendship is often costly. Consider the "friend who sticks closer than a brother," the Lord Jesus Christ. He is the most important friend anyone can have! He is a true friend who has demonstrated His love for you, even when you were not a friend to him. In the story of Jackie Robinson, we would all like to imagine ourselves as Pee Wee Reese, right? But what if you were part of the crowd heckling and hurling insults? How would you feel? That is the situation we found ourselves in with the Lord Jesus. Romans 5:10 puts it this way, "…when we were enemies we were reconciled to God through the death of His Son."

You see, Christ loved you so much that He was willing to die for you even when you were considered His enemy! His enemy? That's right, every one of us is a sinner. (Romans 3:23) Our sin is an affront to a Holy God because sin is the enemy of holiness. But Jesus wants to be our friend, so He provided a way for that to happen by dying in our place on a bloody, cruel cross. He took our place! You know you have a *true* friend when He is willing to die for you! He laid his life down for me and for you demonstrating His incredible love for us! (Romans 5:8)

WALK IN VICTORY... *Consider the C.S. Lewis quote above. How are you adding "value" to someone else's life through true friendship?*

VICTIMS OR VICTORS?

*"What shall we say then? Shall we continue in sin that grace may abound?
Certainly not! How shall we who died to sin live any longer in it?"*

ROMANS 6:1-2

In Romans 6:1-2, a big question arises, "If grace can overcome *ALL* sin at
ALL times, doesn't that give me a free pass to sin? All I have to do is ask for
forgiveness, right?" But the Apostle Paul answers with a resounding, *"NO!"*
The way Paul words it, this is *"The BIGGEST No"* in his eyes! Why would we
choose sin?! Our hearts have been freed and made alive in Christ! We are
slaves to sin no longer! *PRAISE GOD!*

But the heart isn't the only changed thing about us. Paul reminds us that
victory is also a matter of the mind. (vv.3-11) New facts have been introduced
and new thoughts are ready to be learned and experienced in our everyday
lives. We have a new identity by relating to Christ in His death. *"Knowing
["experiencing"]* this, that our old man was crucified with Him…" (6:6a) Our
"old man" has been put to death and we are no longer separated from God—
we are separated from our sin! "For he who has died has been freed from
sin." (6:7) We also have a new identity by relating to Christ in His burial.
"Knowing ["experiencing"] this, …that the body of sin might be done away with,
that we should no longer be slaves of sin." (6:6b) That old way of living has
been buried. He's gone! When Christ arose, the sin stayed dead! Thirdly, we
have a new identity by relating to Christ in His burial. *"Knowing ["experiencing"]*
that Christ, having been raised from the dead, dies no more. Death no longer
has dominion over Him. (6:9) How is this played out? "Likewise you also,
reckon *["do the math"]* yourselves to be dead indeed to sin, but alive to God
in Christ Jesus our Lord." (6:11) It's simple math: Sin = Death; Christ = Life!
You cannot sin and live!

Finally, the victorious life is a matter of the will. (vv.12-14) The heart has
been freed! The mind "knows" the "reckons" these truths. It's time for some
action! Here, Paul introduces us to the matter of "yielding." As we yield our
lives to the Lord Jesus, He uses us as His servants! We *get to* (not "have
to"… *"GET TO!"*) live a life that glorifies God! (vv.12-23) There's a really
simple word for this new way of living—*obedience*. "But God be thanked that
though you were slaves of sin, yet you *obeyed from the heart*…" (6:17, emphasis
added) Your heart has been changed. Your mind knows and reckons the
truths of your new identity. All that's left to do is *LIVE VICTORIOUSLY!*
"But now having been set free from sin, and having become slaves of God,
you have your fruit to holiness, and the end, everlasting life." (6:22)

WALK IN VICTORY *… DO THE MATH! Sin = Death; Christ = Life!*

WALK THIS WAY

"Therefore, be imitators of God as dear children. And walk in love, as Christ also has loved us and given Himself for us, an offering and a sacrifice to God for a sweet-smelling aroma."

EPHESIANS 5:1-2

Time seems to go by so fast and I desperately want to make a difference for the Lord Jesus while I am on this side of eternity. How about you? Several times throughout the year, I renew my resolve to make the most of my time. Redeeming the time by walking with God is a mark of Christian maturity. How can we make the most of our time and walk well with the Lord?

[Read Ephesians 5:1-17]

WALK IN LOVE ... (vv.1-7) As "imitators of God" our lives must reflect the characteristics of our Father. As we walk in love "as dear children," we are characterized by a commitment to our Savior (v.2), a commitment to service (v.2), a commitment to sacrifice (v.2), and a commitment to sanctification. (vv.3-7) As "imitators of God" our walk of love sets up apart from that which is offensive to the Lord we love. (v.6) In this way, a loving walk in an obedient walk because we find no joy or pleasure in sin. Christ's love made him a "friend of sinners," but not a participant in sin. (Matthew 11:19; Luke 7:34; Hebrews 4:15)

WALK IN LIGHT ... (vv.8-14) "For you were once darkness, but now you are light in the Lord. Walk as children of light." As imitators of God, we are called to be light in a dark world. This light is marked by a Spirit-controlled life! (vv.9-10) Notice the fruit of walking in the light: goodness (that is, moral excellence, goodness in thought, word and deed); righteousness (that is, moral integrity, light emanating through right living); and truth (that is, moral reality, honesty and sincerity in living out the Word of God). As we walk in light, we put the dark to shame because light reveals what the darkness conceals! Our walk of light shines so the character, course, and consequences of sin are made clear! (vv.11-14)

WALK IN THE LORD'S LOGIC ... (vv.15-17) The world's insane version of "wisdom" is wildly inconsistent! God's wisdom is careful and consistent. To "walk circumspectly" means walking with godly accuracy, biblical exactness, and logical care. The walk of logic imitates the originator of all wisdom (God Himself). The Lord's logical walk is not careless or self-confident ("not as fools"). In Proverbs, a fool is someone who knows what is right and true but refuses to trust and obey. Instead of following God's wisdom, they are self-confident in their human reasoning, and therefore, careless. The walk of logic complies and complements. In other words, because the Lord's logical walk chooses to trust and obey God's Word, this wise walker complies with God's Word which results in a life that complements God's glory!

WALK IN VICTORY ... *Are you compromising your walk with the Lord through disobedience? (v.6) How do you know you are walking in the Lord's love, light, and logic?*

Check out the results of this wise-walking life in Ephesians 5:17-6:9. (Notice the word "therefore" kicks off this section of practical application!)

WE HAVE THIS TREASURE

"But we have this treasure in earthen vessels, that the excellence of the power may be of God and not of us."

2 CORINTHIANS 4:7

In 1817, Thomas Beale and a group of 30 Virginians ventured west on a hunting expedition. While hunting, they unexpectedly discovered gold near Pike's Peak in Colorado. The gold was carried back and secretly buried in Bedford County, Virginia. Soon after, Beale wrote three ciphers about the treasure's location and content and locked them in a trunk which he entrusted to an innkeeper. Beale never returned for the trunk. To this day, the ciphers remain unsolved and the treasure undiscovered! Beale's treasure is either one of the greatest hoaxes or greatest unsolved challenges yet to be conquered!

In 2 Corinthians 4, the Apostle Paul outlines the beauty of Christ's Gospel in terms of "light" and "treasure." This treasure is no hoax, but it is certainly a great challenge! Paul gives us several "clues" to help point us to the treasure while also showing the price of cheapening its enormous worth.

Costly Surrender ... (4:1) Nothing will distract from the beauty and value of the Gospel than a Christian who constantly says, "I give up!" Many treasure hunters go broke trying to strike it rich. They are willing to sacrifice *everything* because the treasure they seek is so valuable! If you think that's foolish, you should read what Jesus has to say in Matthew 13:44-46.

Covered Shame ... (4:2) We cannot treasure Christ if we treasure sin. And if you think hiding sin isn't the same as "treasuring" it, think again. Deep down, you value this sin and you want to keep it, so you protect it from the revealing light of the Gospel! Covered shame says, "Jesus is *not* enough!"

Compromised Stances ... (4:2-3) Friends, the Gospel ("good news") starts with some bad news. The bad news *will* offend because it's *BAD!* But we cannot change the message out of a spirit of caution or compromise. It does not matter how pleasant the truth is. The truth is *TRUE*. That's all that matters!

Crafty Satan ... (4:3) "If our gospel is veiled, it is veiled to those who are perishing." What a terrible reality! If we "veil" the Gospel through covered shame or compromised stances, we alienate the lost! The enemy tempts us to be cautious about sharing this treasure, but there is treasure enough for all!

Communication of Self ... (4:5a) YOU and I are *not* the good news—Christ is! You do not need the lost world to love you or be convinced of your greatness. They must see the Lord Jesus!

84

Compressed Service … (4:5b) Do you see yourself as a "bondservant for Jesus' sake" as verse 5 declares? Do your actions and attitudes show that the Lord Jesus is your Master? Does Christ call the shots in your life? Or have you compressed your hours of service to whenever it is convenient for you?

Commanded to Shine … (4:6) God has given us the glorious light of the Gospel to SHINE OUT the message of the Lord Jesus Christ! This treasure glitters brightly if you shine boldly as a willing servant of the Lord!

WALK IN VICTORY … *Is the life of Christ a precious treasure to you? Are you magnifying the beauty of the treasure or diminishing its value through your actions? If you didn't already, go read the parable Jesus uses in Matthew 13:44-46.*

WHAT IS YOUR LIFE?

"Whereas you do not know what will happen tomorrow. For what is your life? It is even a vapor that appears for a little time and then vanishes away."

JAMES 4:14

There is an advertisement that says, "Life is short, play hard." It has some truth to it! Life is short and unpredictable, so it is best to do everything you do (working, playing, serving the Lord, etc.) with maximum effort! As you grow older, you start to realize that life is getting shorter every day. For some, this mid-life crisis drives them to adopt the "play hard" mantra. But I think there's a better answer to the brevity of life: "Live with eternity in mind!"

James 4:14 says, "Whereas you do not know what will happen tomorrow. For what is your life? It is even a vapor that appears for a little time and then vanishes away." This verse might seem sad at first glance, but it is packed with deep meaning and great application for every stage of life! Today we will discuss three issues raised in this verse:

The Issue of Trusting God – The first thing I notice is the issue of trusting God with your future. Yes, making plans and setting goals for your life is important, but the *most* important thing is to make sure your plans and goals are grounded in the Lord. You don't know what the future holds, but God certainly does! You do not know what will happen tomorrow, next week, or 10 years from now, but God does! Will you trust Him? King David once wrote in Psalm 16:1, "Preserve me, O God, for in You I put my trust." There is great comfort and confidence in trusting the Lord to preserve you and establish your future.

The Issue of Your Life – The second thing I notice is the question, "What is your life?" The Lord has given each one of us only ONE LIFE to live! That is a sobering thought. The question we must ask ourselves is, "What will I do with the ONE LIFE God has given me?" Our gracious Lord has demonstrated His great love for us by giving us abundant, eternal life. That life was not given to make it all about us—it is *all about Him*!

The Issue of Time – The last thing I see in this verse is that we don't have much time to accomplish the task! Our lives are so short compared to eternity. The Bible tells us in Ephesians 5:15-16, "See then that you walk circumspectly (precisely, carefully), not as fools but as wise, redeeming the time, because the days are evil." The days in which we live are certainly evil, so we have no time to waste! Determine now to live every moment *circumspectly*—with attentive, careful precision—completely consumed by glorifying the Lord!

WALK IN VICTORY ... *Are you living with attentive, careful precision today?*

WHO'S YOUR DADDY?

"You are of your father the devil ... for he is a liar and the father of it."

JOHN 8:44

My father's name was Stanley Winfrey Long. My name is Stanley Winfrey Long II. My oldest son's name is Stanley Winfrey Long III. (We call him "Buddy.") Why do Buddy and I have those Roman numerals behind our names? Was that just a cool add-on to our birth certificates? Not at all! We share a name with our father. In fact, Buddy shares many characteristics with his earthly father—looks, mannerisms, speech, etc. In the past, I've played a trick on people where I show them a picture of me when I was a kid and say, "Hey, look at this picture of Buddy!" That little trick has stumped more than a few people because he looks a lot like his father.

One day, Jesus was talking to a group of religious people and He told them they were displaying the characteristics of their spiritual father—the devil! Whoa—wait a minute, Jesus! The people You are talking to say they love God, they honor God, and they serve God! They might *think* that way, but in another passage, Jesus has this to say about that group of phonies, "These people draw near to Me with their mouth, and honor Me with their lips, but their heart is far from Me. And in vain they worship Me..." (Matthew 15:8-9) What a brutal accusation from the Lord Jesus Himself!

It seems like everyone I meet "believes in God" and is "on their way to Heaven." But the Bible doesn't seem to agree. The Bible says that even demons believe in God and tremble before Him, and they are definitely NOT going to heaven! (James 2:19) How can you know you are *truly* a child of God? The Bible makes it clear—you can tell who's your daddy by the actions and attitudes that consistently characterize your life. So how can I know? While the Apostle Paul offers many lengthy lists of contrasting ways of life, we will summarize his list from Galatians 5:19-26 into a brief outline:

A Child of Satan... (vv.19-21)	*A Child of God... (vv.22-26)*	
– Sexual immorality (v.19)	+ Love	+ Goodness
– Submitting to ungodly power (v.20)	+ Joy	+ Faithfulness
– Systemic hatred of others (vv.20-21)	+ Peace	+ Gentleness
– Slaves to pleasure (v.21)	+ Patience	+ Kindness
– Slaves to substance (v.21)	+ Self-Control	

WALK IN VICTORY ... *Based on these lists, Who's Your Daddy? Do you resemble your Heavenly Father or someone else entirely?*

THE BIG DEAL ABOUT LYING

"Lying lips are an abomination to the Lord, but those who deal truthfully are His delight."

PROVERBS 12:22

Does God really concern Himself with every exaggeration, "white lie," or partial truth? Not too long ago I heard about a discussion about lying which took place in a Christian college's ethics class. Apparently, even at a Christian college, the debate was fierce and the conclusion was not so cut and dry! Lying might be a big part of today's world, and "situational ethics" might be all the rage, but if you think lying is okay, you are only lying to yourself!

What's the big deal about lying? According to John 8:31-32 and 8:44, we know the origins of truth and lying (to be purposefully "anti-truth"). Anti-truth originated with Satan, the "father of lies" (John 8:44), and truth is Who God is! (John 8:31-32) We are never more like Satan than when we lie because we have adopted his native language! Lying reflects Satan's lust for power and control. This goes back to the Garden of Eden when he told Eve, "You will not surely die… your eyes will be opened, and you will be like God…" (Genesis 3:4) Lying is often an attempt to control a narrative, a situation, or perception. It makes us feel powerful over anyone willing to believe our fabrication.

Lying is condemned by God as sin because it is anti-truth, and therefore, anti-God. (Exodus 20:16) Living anti-truth is one of the things God "hates" in Proverbs 6:16-19. In fact, of the seven "abominations" listed in this passage, at least three of these actions have their root in falsehood of some kind. To this end, you can be sure that lying will be judged harshly by God. God's "Hall of Shame" in Revelation 21:8 tells us "all liars" (that is, those who continue to act like their father, Satan) are cast into the lake of fire!

Lying reveals our obsession with self and opposition to the Savior. We lie to satisfy our selfish desires. This is the very essence of the "I'm in charge" attitude. This kind of attitude opposes our great Savior! (John 8:45) A liar spits in the face of Truth Himself (John 14:6) and rejects the truths of God's Word. (John 17:17) To live in a spirit of "anti-truth" is dangerous because it will always spiral out of control. Lies tend to multiply as one lie usually leads to another. Lies also manipulate as we have to rewrite stories, memories, and circumstances to keep them covered up. Lies also manifest our bondage into other people's lives. Where the Holy Spirit wants to give freedom and life through truth our lies stink of the curse and shame of death. Lying makes you a weapon in the hands of the enemy! Lying is a *BIG* deal!

WALK IN VICTORY *… Do you take the anti-God nature of lying seriously?*

WHO APPROVED THIS?!

"For do I now persuade men, or God? Or do I seek to please men? For if I still pleased men, I would not be a bondservant of Christ."

GALATIANS 1:10

"Who approved this?!" That is not a question you ever want to hear from your boss! Someone overstepped. Someone without the authority to authorize has placed their stamp of approval in the space left for the boss. We might ask, "Why would you ever move ahead without the boss's approval?" That's a good question! Are we asking that same question about our walk with God?

Seeking approval is a natural part of our human nature. Nothing feels better than a pat on the back and a "Well done!" from someone in authority. Few feelings outweigh the joy of making an entire room of people laugh because we made a great joke, or nod approvingly at a profound statement. But the approval of man is a trap! (Proverbs 29:25) Constantly seeking the approval of others can make us freeze, frustrated, or put us into a frenzy!

We freeze when we refuse to do anything until we know how it will be received by others. If we want the people around us to approve everything we do before we act, we will spend a lifetime doing nothing. We become frustrated because the approval of man is a moving target. One day, that joke makes them laugh, but the next day *you* become the punchline! There is nothing more frustrating than attempting to please people who constantly change their minds. The approval of man puts us into a frenzy when we attempt to constantly chase their approval. The feeling of "I will never be enough" is the direct result of desperately chasing the approval of man.

What about God's approval? Paul tells us in Galatians 1:10, "For do I now persuade men, or God? Or do I seek to please men? For if I still pleased men, I would not be a bondservant of Christ." This solves the problems of freezing, frustration, and frenzy! With the Holy Spirit of God within us, we always have direction. There is never a need to freeze and wait for permission to do His will! There is no more frustration because God's will is anything but a moving target—it is clear, unchanging, and anchored in Christ! There is no frenzy when seeking God's approval either. Paul reassures us in Philippians 4:7, "And the peace of God, which surpasses all understanding, will guard your hearts and minds through Christ Jesus." In other words, to be in the will of God is to dwell in God's overwhelming peace!

WALK IN VICTORY ... *Are you frozen, frustrated, or frenzied by seeking the approval of man or enjoying the peace and confidence of God's approval?*

WHY DO CHRISTIANS SUFFER?

"From the Jews five times I received forty stripes minus one. Three times I was beaten with rods; once I was stoned; three times I was shipwrecked; a night and a day I have been in the deep; in journeys often, in perils of waters, in perils of robbers, in perils of my own countrymen, in perils of the Gentiles, in perils in the city, in perils in the wilderness, in perils in the sea, in perils among false brethren; in weariness and toil, in sleeplessness often, in hunger and thirst, in fastings often, in cold and nakedness…"

2 CORINTHIANS 11:24-27

Are Christians supposed to suffer? Some believe Christians are supposed to always have it easy! Sermons on suffering can be rare because suffering is a topic we would rather avoid. I mean, who enjoys talking about suffering? My friend, suffering is a mighty tool in God's hands! God redeems suffering to conform us to His Son, and the way we respond to suffering can be a detriment or a benefit toward this transformation. Let's briefly examine three ways God uses suffering in the Christian life.

SUFFERING TEACHES ME ABOUT CHRIST … Suffering helps us understand and know the Lord more. No one suffered more than our Lord! Suffering can help us realize the pain that Christ endured for our salvation. Suffering then becomes a tool to help us understand Christ's love! Our suffering, compared to His, is minimal. Suffering moves us from knowing *about* God to *experiencing* Him. (Job 42:5)

SUFFERING IDENTIFIES ME WITH CHRIST … Jesus said in John 15:20, "The servant is not greater than his Lord…" In other words, since Christ suffered, why wouldn't we? Suffering brings us to a place of identification with Christ. We identify with His death, and as a result, get to identify with His life! (Galatians 2:20) Paul looked at suffering, specifically persecution for the cause of Christ, as a badge of honor! Paul had the *privilege* of being identified with Christ through "the fellowship of His sufferings." (Philippians 3:10) Are you willing to be identified with Christ through hardship and suffering? Do you love Christ that much? (2 Timothy 2:2, 3:12)

SUFFERING MAKES ME LIKE CHRIST … Suffering purges our self-sufficiency so we might be wholly dependent upon Christ! Suffering draws us into deeper intimacy with the Lord because as we suffer, we want to be closer to the Lord—it's only natural to pursue His power and comfort in hardship! A detrimental response to suffering will bring bitterness, anger, resentment, compromise, and fear. A right response to suffering will make us like Christ as we draw near for help. (Psalm 145:18; Hebrews 10:19-23)

WALK IN VICTORY … *How are you responding to suffering in your life right now?*

WILL YOU STAND?

"… for by faith you stand."

2 CORINTHIANS 1:24

I have had the privilege of serving in the Christian camp ministry for many years. In that time, I have witnessed the Lord do an incredible, life-changing work in the lives of many young people! Countless lives have been changed through the ministry of Christian camps because campers encounter the Lord Jesus through His creation and His Word. By God's grace, I have seen many positive spiritual decisions take place at camp, but what happens to these spiritual decisions when the camper arrives back home? What happens when they unplug from the *REAL* world of God's creation and God's Word? I pray these campers learn to *STAND!*

Standing is usually seen as a positive, proactive response. It signals "readiness." As a posture, it is affirming, respectful, and active. One who is standing is holding their ground and ready for action! The Bible's command to stand has some great spiritual and practical applications for the victorious Christian life. "To stand" means you have your feet firmly planted on a solid foundation, and you are ready for the assault of the enemy. But what does look like practically to stand by faith?

Stand in Liberty by Living in the Power of God … Galatians 5:1 – Liberty is one of the great marks of victory! You cannot have a victorious Christian life without freedom from sin, and true liberty *only* comes from living in the power of God! "Christ has made us free…" means Christ does the liberating. "Do not be entangled again…" means it is time for us to *choose* to live in the freedom won by Christ!

Stand in Love by Living in the Person of God … Philippians 4:1 – Love for the Lord and love for others is a firm foundation on which to stand! Living in the person of God (John 15:4) gives you the proper priorities of life (see Matthew 22:36-40; Galatians 5:14) and keeps the enemy from knocking you down.

Stand in Labor by Living in the Purpose of God … 1 Corinthians 15:58 – Every saved person is called by God to labor in the purpose designed by God! You do not have to manufacture your purpose through success or power or accomplishments—you simply do what He designed you to do. (Ephesians 2:8-10)

WALK IN VICTORY … *Meditate on Paul's "stand" verses: Philippians 1:27; 1 Corinthians 15:1, 16:13; 2 Corinthians 1:24; Galatians 5:1; Ephesians 6:10-17*

WITH CHRIST, IT'S *OVER!*

"Then behold, men brought on a bed a man who was paralyzed, whom they sought to bring in and lay before Him. And when they could not find how they might bring him in, because of the crowd, they went up on the housetop and let him down with his bed through the tiling into the midst before Jesus."

LUKE 5:18-19

In Luke 5:17-26, we are treated to a fascinating story about some faith-filled friends who brought a paralyzed man to Jesus, and the cold response of the jealous religious leaders. Luke tells us, "And the power of the Lord was present to heal them." (v.17) The people gathered with an *overly expectant* belief that the Lord was going to move in a life-changing way! They were confident in the person of the Lord Jesus Christ. They knew He was more than ordinary—they were *overly expectant* for a good reason!

"Then behold, men brought on a bed a man who was paralyzed … they went up on the housetop and let him down with his bed through the tiling into the midst before Jesus." (vv.18-19) What a visual! These men were so *overly concerned* about their friend that they went to extreme lengths to get their friend to Jesus! They were resolved and determined to get him to the Savior no matter what! Where did this resolve come from? Verse 20 says, "And when Jesus saw their faith…" Yes! Not the paralyzed man's faith, but *their* faith! Are we so *overly concerned* for the lost that we are willing to exercise incredible "take the roof off" faith in getting our friends and family to Jesus?

Look at the response our Lord. "Man, your sins are forgiven you." (v.20) Isn't that just like our Lord to do *over and beyond* what is asked of Him? *WHAT A GREAT SAVIOR!* (Ephesians 3:20-21) An encounter with Jesus is more than a "touch"—it is a transformation! If Jesus is willing to go *over and beyond* what was asked of Him, we need to be willing to do the same! We need to be in our community touching, serving, loving, giving—and most importantly—telling folks about Jesus!

Sadly, we cannot expect this overabundance of goodness to go without opposition! Here comes the *overly critical* response: "Who is this who speaks blasphemies? Who can forgive sins but God alone?" (v.21) Notice, you don't see these guys bringing friends to Jesus through the roof. Instead, they sit back and faithlessly complain. Constructive criticism can be a good thing, but these guys are trying to find fault. The *overly critical* will always appear where God is at work! We cannot give them our attention.

Jesus does what I could not do and responds in an *overly gracious* way. (See vv.22-25) He graciously supports His claim to forgive sins by healing the man's paralysis. And how did the people respond? The crowd is *overwhelmed!* "And they were all amazed, and they glorified God and were filled with fear…" (v.26) The message of Jesus will always produce *over-the-top* responses. With Christ, the *overflow* is joy!

WALK IN VICTORY … *Are you noticing the work of God around you? Are you responding positively or critically to God's work around you? Are you joining God's Work around you?*

WORMOLOGY

"But I am a worm, and no man; A reproach of men, and despised by the people."

PSALM 22:6

Psalm 22 is a Messianic Psalm sometimes referred to as the "fifth Gospel." In it, King David uses the worm as an illustration of a man who is broken, suffering, and a "reproach of men." (v.6) As redneck theologian who loves fishing, the worm gives me several simple reminders for the eradication of self in our walk with the Lord. I call this illustration "Wormology."

A Worm is Powerless – A Christian has no real strength outside of the power of God. Christians must abandon the "Little Engine" mentality of "I think I can, I think I can." Our confidence is not in our willpower, but in a life surrendered to the Lord and His power! (Philippians 4:13) Real power in the Christian life is a post-mortem reality—you have to die first! (Romans 6:11)

A Worm Craves Moisture – Like the worm needs moisture, Christians need the water of God's Word. Psalm 1:2-3 tells us that the blessed man of God is like a tree planted on a riverbank whose roots drink deeply from the nearby stream. A man blessed by the refreshing water of God's Word is fruitful and never dries up! "Whatever he does shall prosper." (Psalm 1:3) What a promise! On the other hand, a Christian without the moisture of the Word will dry up like a worm on a summer sidewalk.

A Worm is Willingly Crushed – A worm might look like little a snake, but its nature is completely different. You will never see a worm wind up to strike when it is about to be crushed. A Christian should endure hardship for the sake of doing what is right. After all, this is how the Lord Jesus lived as an expression of humble obedience. You can often tell who is in charge of a person's heart by the way he reacts to being crushed by others!

A Worm Stretches for the Goal – If you ever watch a worm inch its way across the ground, it must stretch its body in order to move. Sometimes, those stretches look pretty uncomfortable! It takes a lot of effort for a worm to move around. A Christian who wants to get anywhere spiritually should be willing for the Lord to stretch him out of his comfort zone because, comfortable or uncomfortable, Christ is a worthy prize! (Philippians 3:12-14)

A Worm is Renewed After Being Broken – Life is hard and we are often broken through circumstances or God's careful plan of renewal. Like a worm who regenerates after being broken, a Christian must be broken for the self-life to be replaced by the Christ-life. (Galatians 2:20; Romans 6:16-18)

A Worm Knows its Place in the Dirt – The Word of God reminds us that our origin is found in the dirt. (Genesis 2:7; Psalm 103:14) You will never see a worm in an elevated place unless someone else put it there. Similarly, it is Christ's life that elevates man from dirt to sons of God! (1 John 3:1-2) No amount of effort or willpower could elevate our status in this way. It is only possible by God's amazing grace!

A Worm is Good for Fishing – "Follow Me, and I will make you become fishers of men." (Mark 1:17) The Lord Jesus Christ has called us to be fishers of men! Though we know and recognize our humble origins in the dirt, we have been called up and called out to go fishing for souls!

A Worm Affects its Environment – As a worm moves through the dirt, it fertilizes the ground and provides nutrients to enrich its environment. God has given each one of us a sphere of influence, and as we daily die to self, the Lord will use us to continually affect our environment for the glory of God.

WALK IN VICTORY ... *Which characteristics of Wormology are missing in your walk with God?*

> *"Lord, bend that proud and stiff-necked I, Help me to bow the head and die;*
> *Beholding Him on Calvary, Who bowed His head for me."* — Roy Hession

ZACCHAEUS: LITTLE GUY, BIG PROBLEM!

"Zacchaeus, make haste and come down, for today I must stay at your house."

LUKE 19:5

I love using the story of Zacchaeus to introduce kids to the Lord! I almost always use this story whenever we have our weekend overnighters at Camp Eagle. Like many kids, Zacchaeus was a little guy with a BIG problem! No, it wasn't his height—it was his heart. Zacchaeus had heard about Jesus and wanted to see for himself if the rumors about this amazing man were true! Zacchaeus went out of his way to see for himself who Jesus was. You might know someone like Zacchaeus today. They may have heard about Jesus and they are curious if the word going around is true. Let me encourage you to go out of your way to help them find out about this man called Jesus!

I am sure Zacchaeus did not plan to meet or converse with Jesus. I'm convinced that his curiosity would have been satisfied with a tree-top view, but you cannot get that close to Truth Himself without the Truth pressing its weight on your heart and mind. Zacchaeus was met with a point of decision! The Lord graciously met Lil' Zac exactly where he was. "When Jesus came to the place, He looked up and saw him…" Jesus knew the place. He knew when to stop, and He knew when to look up. And you know what, Jesus knows exactly where you are, too! When we are confronted with Jesus, we are faced with a choice: "What will I do with this man named Jesus?" (And on the flip-side, what will Jesus do with *me*?) I'm sure Lil' Zac was worried about what someone like Jesus might do to a no-good, double-dealing thief!

So what happened? "Zacchaeus, make haste and come down, for today I must stay at your house." (v.5) Jesus is coming over for dinner! Zacchaeus didn't hesitate—he humbled himself. Zacchaeus may have been a despised man, but he responded to the Lord's invitation without fear of what other people might think. Zacchaeus was happy to come to Jesus!

Everyone knew Lil' Zac was a little guy with a BIG heart problem. (v.7) But in the presence of the Lord, Zacchaeus was a changed man! "Look, Lord, I give half of my goods to the poor; and if I have taken anything from anyone by false accusation, I restore fourfold." (v.8) When Zacchaeus trusted Christ, this once-greedy little man with a BIG heart problem completely changed! The same is true for anyone who comes to the Lord by faith! "For the Son of Man has come to seek and to save that which was lost." (v.10)

WALK IN VICTORY … *What will you do with Jesus? More importantly, what does Jesus want to do with you?*

REMEMBERING: A GENERATIONAL GIFT

"Choose for yourselves this day whom you will serve…
But as for me and my house, we will serve the Lord."

JOSHUA 24:15

"And the people said to Joshua, 'The Lord our God we will serve, and His voice we will obey!'" This declaration was Israel's response to Joshua's farewell address in Joshua 23 and 24. Unfortunately, things change quickly. Judges 2 tells us, "So the people served the Lord all the days of Joshua, and all the days of the elders who outlived Joshua, who had seen all the great works of the Lord which He had done for Israel. When [Joshua's] generation had been gathered to their fathers, another generation arose after them who did not know the Lord nor the work which He had done for Israel. Then the children of Israel did evil in the sight of the Lord…and they forsook the Lord God of their fathers." (vv.7,10-12) How did this falling away happen so fast? Are we on the same track right now? How do we—the Joshua generation—rescue the next generation from abandoning the Lord?

Remember God's Victories … (Joshua 23:3-5) God had promised Israel an inheritance, but enemies stood in the way. God defeated these enemies as Israel acted in faith and obeyed His command to fight! We must remember that we serve a victorious God! He is undefeated! Every promised inheritance is realized by those who live by faith. (Ephesians 1:18-19; 1 Peter 1:4-5)

Remember God's Promises … (Joshua 23:6-9) God promised to bless Israel as long as they remained loyal to the Lord. Remembering God's promises will guard us against fear and keep us from sin as we live in Christ. (2 Peter 1:4)

Remember God's Love for You … (Joshua 23:10-13) God demanded loyalty because God is loyal to His people. Freedom is found in the loyal love of God. He will not forsake us, so do not forsake our freedom! (Galatians 5:1)

Remember God's Faithful Goodness … (Joshua 23:13-16) God is faithful and His goodness is unchanging. This is a great comfort to our hearts! God's good favor to Israel was an unearned gift, and the same is true for us! (Psalm 23:6)

Remember God Offers a Choice … (Joshua 24:14-27) Joshua points out the only logical choice—*SERVE THE LORD!* As we remember what God has done for us, is there any other choice? Instead of trying to find satisfaction and acceptance somewhere else, purpose to be set apart for God's glory!

WALK IN VICTORY … *Older believer: How are you helping younger believers remember God? Younger believer: Do you have an older believer helping you remember?*

VICTORY!

ABOUT THE AUTHOR

Stanley W. Long II went to be with his Lord and Savior on Saturday, September 15, 2018. Though we were shocked, the Lord was not. Stanley finished his race well, and this book is a testimony to a life well lived and a race well run. Stanley was saved by God's grace at the age of 12 and dedicated his life to sharing the hope and truth of the victorious Gospel with thousands of people through the ministries of Camp Eagle and Shenandoah Baptist Church, where he served since 2000.

Stanley was a devoted husband to his wife, Kelle, an amazing dad to his kids, Lindsey, Kassie, Meredith, Emily, Miriam, Buddy, Abby, Asa, and Ezra, and a fun-loving Pops to his grandkids. We miss him dearly, but we do not grieve without hope! We know Stanley is worshipping in the presence of his victorious Savior, the Lord Jesus Christ, and we will see him again!

The devotionals in this book are a collection of Stan's teaching over the years based on his personal sermon notes, devotional writings, audio sermons, and a collection of handwritten notes from friends who sat under his teaching.

Stanley's handwritten VICTORY! can be seen throughout the pages of this book as a testimony to his most repeated teaching. He would be thrilled to know this theme is the legacy of his faithful biblical instruction!

To learn how you can invest in eternity and help support the ongoing ministry of Camp Eagle, please visit them online at:

https://campeagleva.org/donate

Made in the USA
Middletown, DE
13 October 2023

40724364R00064